# creating
## a container
# garden

# creating
# a container
# garden

*p*

This is a Parragon Book
First published in 2002

Parragon
Queen Street House
4 Queen Street
Bath BA1 1HE, UK
Copyright © Parragon 2002

ISBN: 0-75257-440-X

A CIP data record for this book is available from the British Library.

Created and designed by
Foundry Design and Production.

**Acknowledgements**
Text: Deena Beverley and Barty Phillips
Illustrations: Kate Simunek
Special photography: Andrew Newton-Cox

Printed in China

WARNING: Some of the projects in this book include electrically powered pumps and every effort has been made to
recommend the safest way of installing them. When buying the electrical components for any project, always check
that they are designed to be used in water. If in doubt at any stage, seek the advice of a qualified electrician. Advice is
also given on child safety and every effort has been made to ensure that this information is correct. It should be
noted, however, that children can drown in even very shallow depths of water and must not be left unsupervised near
a water feature. The publishers and the author cannot accept any legal responsibility or liability for accidents incurred
as a result of the construction of any of the projects described in this book.

# CONTENTS

❦

# INTRODUCTION

❦

Container gardening now offers more scope for inventiveness than
ever before, for two reasons – the range of plants suitable for
growing in pots has grown so much that it even includes small fruit trees,
while the choice of wonderful containers is seemingly endless.
With a little flair and imagination, almost anything can be used
as an attractive receptacle for your favourite plants.

❀

With a little careful planning, a container garden can progress through the
seasons with as much colour and interest as a 'conventional' garden,
starting with the bulbs that celebrate the arrival of spring, moving
through the colours and scents of summer flowers, and ending with
autumnal hues and winter-flowering shrubs.

❀

Climbing plants, dwarf specimen trees, roses, ferns, ornamental grasses,
herbs and even vegetables can be grown in containers. And if you feel like
a change, container gardening has the advantage, as pots can be rearranged
or replanted to create a totally new look.

❀

In the following chapters you will find plenty of practical advice
and tips, not only on selecting plants and containers but also on
how to create the right garden to show off your containers.
This includes information on planning roof gardens, how to
build hard surfaces, such as patios, how to use garden lighting
to good effect, how to establish attractive and practical garden
boundaries and how to build a pond. There is also a selection of
pots and planters projects to liven up your garden.

# GARDENING IN CONTAINERS

**Choosing your container or collection of containers is part of the fun of this type of gardening, but whatever you select should match the style of garden.**

❖

Rustic containers look great in cottage gardens, for example, but formal gardens need a more elegant style of pot. And if you choose a heavy pot or a sink, you need to be sure that you are happy with its position before you plant it up, as moving it later will be difficult.

❖

The next task is choosing what to plant, and there are ideas in this chapter that will provide interest throughout the year.

❖

Container gardening is perfect for roof gardens and balconies, although there are special considerations here – lightweight pots and compost are a must, and there may be other potential pitfalls, such as structural limitations. And if all you have is a window, then plant up a fantastic window box!

# CONTAINER GARDENS

Pots and containers can be used to provide visual interest throughout the year; the most sculptural ones need have nothing planted in them at all. They can be moved around to fill gaps, rearrange the balance of some aspect of the garden, or add a particular colour. Used for tender plants, they can stand outside in summer and be brought inside during cold weather. Pots can also be used to hold climbers to enhance patios, terraces, balconies, courtyards and windowsills. They can be used to revitalise dull areas and introduce interest to the bleakest of tiny alleyways or basement areas.

## CHOOSING CONTAINERS

THE range of possible containers is enormous. Almost anything can be used as a container, provided it has drainage holes and will hold enough compost to support the plant. Many are purpose made but there is plenty of scope for using containers not originally intended for plants, and these may be equally effective and cheaper. In Greece, for example, brightly painted old paint cans filled with red pelargoniums are often ranged along the street wall of whitewashed cottages.

❀ Old chimney pots can be simple in shape or very decorative and will add height where it may be needed.
❀ Wheelbarrows have become popular as containers, although definitely not for formal gardens, and old watering cans, buckets and pails, ceramic sinks and ancient water tanks are all possibilities.

ABOVE: *Chimney pots make interesting containers and you can experiment with plants to see which suit the style of pot best. Here, a fuchsia seems to be enjoying the shaft of sunlight coming in through the door.*

❀ Sinks are very heavy; once positioned you will not want to move one again. Shallow sinks are good for rock garden plants, miniature bulbs and dwarf conifers. White, glazed fire clay sinks can be covered in a substance known as 'tufa' to look just like stone. Alternatively, you can bury a sink in the ground, having first blocked up the plughole, and use it as a miniature bog garden for moisture-loving plants such as primulas.

LEFT: *A brightly painted container garden on different levels provides a colourful entrance to a seaside house.*

## Other choices

❀ Cement-based artificial stone or plain cement planters can look handsome. Large concrete and timber planting cases and barrels can hold enough compost to support a small tree. In the eighteenth century, square or circular wooden tubs planted with orange and lemon trees were placed in rows in formal gardens and taken into an early form of conservatory, or 'orangery', over the winter.

❀ Plastic containers are very much lighter to lift than most other planters, which is a great advantage if you want to move them around. They do not look quite like terracotta but once full of plants and sitting on a patio, the containers themselves will not be very noticeable.

## Clay pots

❀ Clay pots and containers come in a great variety of sizes and designs. Small and medium-sized pots are best grouped together because just one can look a little pathetic on its own in an open space. Very large, shapely ones can be used as ornaments in their own right at the end of an axis or some other prominent place.

❀ Clay pots can vary in colour from cream and pale pink to deep red and a rather brash orange. The colour will weather in time. Choose a relatively simple design so as not to distract attention away from the plants.

❀ Elaborate pots are really suitable only for special situations. Chinese-style pots with coloured glazes are available in useful, sturdy shapes. It is best to choose the same type and colour for pots that are going to be placed in the same area. Check that the pots you buy are frostproof.

BELOW: *This small courtyard garden has been laid with crazy paving and planted with large and small pots of plants to provide interest all year round. There are clipped evergreens for winter interest, pots of geraniums and busy Lizzies that will need to be taken in during the winter, and one or two tall shrubs to soften the edges.*

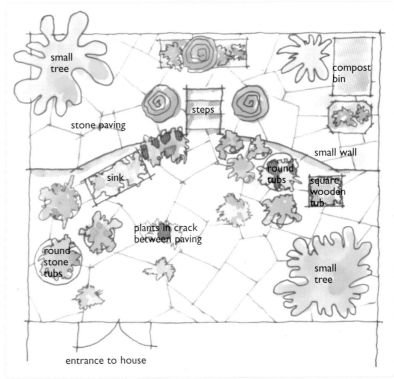

LEFT: *This bold display of Agaves and cacti in pots works particularly well because the stripy spirals of the pots are repeated throughout the area. The low-growing shrubs at the back create an informal low hedge that softens the fence.*

❀ Wallflowers (*Cheiranthus cheiri*) have the most wonderful scent in the late spring garden. Grow them with tulips and daffodils for a rich tapestry of colours. Tulips also look good underplanted with forget-me-nots (*Myosotis*), scillas and grape hyacinths.

❀ Polyanthus are excellent contenders for pots, too. Plant them with pansies or small trumpet daffodils and grape hyacinths. Their colours are wonderful. You can grow the whole palette of colours together, or try the blues and whites as a combination, or blues and pinks and so on. Double daisies (*Bellis perennis*) make good perimeter plants and associate well with forget-me-nots, wallflowers and pansies.

### Planting for summer

❀ There are many interesting and colourful plants for summer containers. Variegated or silvery trailing plants such as small ivies, *Helichrysum petiolare* and *Senecio maritima* 'Silver Dust' can enhance any mixed planting. Useful summer bedding plants include busy Lizzies (for shady places), petunias, verbenas, *Felicia amelloides* and lobelias.

## PLANTS FOR CONTAINERS

As with all design, keep your planting schemes simple. Do not try to mix too many different varieties. Opt for just two or three that will bloom in succession to give a long season of colour. One variety to a pot often looks best of all. You can juxtapose the containers for their colour combinations after planting.

### Planting for spring

❀ Fairly shallow containers with wide tops look great with low-growing spring bulbs such as crocuses and scillas. Taller containers can take taller stemmed plants such as daffodils and tulips. A long-lasting and attractive display can be made with crocuses and iris together with later-flowering tulips and daffodils in a container deep enough to take two levels of bulbs.

❀ Plant the tulips and daffodils at the lowest level. The satiny, almost black tulip, 'Queen of the Night', or a group of elegant lily-flowered tulips such as the snowy 'White Triumphator' are good container bulbs. For daffodils you could try 'Minnow', which has delicate creamy yellow flowers, two to four on a stem. 'Hawera', with pretty yellow heads, is one of the latest-flowering daffodils.

❀ Plant *Iris reticulata* and early crocuses higher up in the compost – when these die down, their leaves will not be noticed because the interest will have moved to the daffodils and tulips. These tiny irises have an upright habit and long slender leaves and look very good grown on their own in pots, although their season is not very long.

BELOW: *In this peaceful water garden, evergreen plants have been used to provide interest at all times of the year, but the summer planting of brightly coloured rock roses in tubs gives it a cheerful feeling in the sun.*

LEFT: *A hot climate is just right for a cactus garden like this one. The garden walls have been painted white and accentuate the shadows of the pots. Even the dog seems to enjoy the sun.*

## Acid-loving plants

❀ Containers can be particularly useful for growing plants for which the soil in your garden is not suitable. Acid-loving plants such as dwarf rhododendrons, azaleas, camellias and heathers can be planted in ericaceous compost. Most of these are woodland plants and prefer not to be in full sun. All have shallow rooting systems, which makes them particularly suitable for container planting.

❀ Pots and pelargoniums might have been made for each other. Use them in window boxes and any other container on their own. Unlike busy Lizzies (*Impatiens*), pelargoniums like strong light. Their foliage has an amazing range of scents, from lemon and peppermint to apple, pine and rose so you can place pots where the aromatic foliage will send out its scent as soon as someone brushes against it.

### Planting for autumn and winter

❀ All clipped evergreen shrubs look good in winter, providing pattern and structure when everything else is over. The common snowdrop (*Galanthus nivalis*) is a hardy bulb not often grown in containers, but it will make a brave show of white and green from late winter to early spring. Flowering shrubs can provide interest, too, especially near the house, since during winter the garden will mostly be seen only from inside.

❀ The small deciduous shrub *Ceratostigma willmottianum* can be planted on its own in a medium-sized pot. It has bright blue flowers all through summer and well into autumn, when its leaves turn red. *Daphne odora* is an evergreen shrub with glossy dark green leaves and clusters of fragrant purplish-pink and white flowers from midwinter to spring. The heather families (*Calluna, Daboecia* and *Erica*) contain species and cultivars that will flower all year. Good winter ones include *Erica* x *darleyensis* 'White Perfection', *E.* x *veitchii* 'Pink Joy' and *E. carnea* 'Vivellii' (bright pink).

BELOW: *The succulent plants in these terracotta pots introduce a variety of shapes that are set off against the sun's shadow on the painted fencing behind them.*

# ROOF GARDENS

A roof garden can be one of the biggest luxuries of city life. It is a true extension of the indoor living space, offering spectacular views over rooftops with a feeling of light and space normally unavailable in the urban environment. It also offers a great location for planted up tubs and pots.

## HISTORY

THE roof garden has a long history. The Hanging Gardens of Babylon were really roof gardens, built over an arcaded palace in ascending terraces. On top of the arches, bundles of reeds and asphalt were laid and covered with brick tiles and thick sheets of lead to provide waterproofing for the decorated state rooms below. Water was raised up by pump. The whole thing was planted with flowering shrubs and trees such as larch, birch, cypress, cedar, acacia and mimosa.

❀ When Derry and Tom's department store was built in London in the 1930s, permission for a further storey was refused because the firemen's ladders were too short to reach it, so a roof garden was built instead. This was made up of a series of traditional gardens including a Hispano-Moorish garden, a Tudor garden and a woodland area complete with a small stream filled with fish and ducks. There was even a cascade and grotto. The garden is still open to the public, and although the introduction of flamingos has led to damage of some vegetation and loss of fish, it is still a magical place to visit and hard to imagine you are among the rooftops.

ABOVE: *This tiny roof space is a haven among the chimney pots in central London. The permanent planting is evergreen, while annuals are grown in tubs for summer interest.*

### Practical difficulties

❀ Recent developments in waterproofing technology and materials and increased roof insulation have made the roof garden a possibility for anyone with a flat roof, and the luxury of extra living space in a small city flat cannot be overemphasised.

❀ Before you begin stocking your lofty garden with plants, there are a number of practical difficulties you should be aware of. Most roofs have a limited load-bearing capacity and may not be able to support the extra weight of surfacing materials, soil, containers and so on. You

LEFT: *This little London roof garden is not only attractive to sit in, but also pretty when seen from the street and the houses opposite. The planting is mostly shrubby and provides interest all year round.*

ABOVE: *On this extremely stylish roof garden, trellis has been used to form an outdoor 'room', creating a space with a Japanese flavour – open to the sky but concealed from the world.*

## Room-like spaces

✿ High up spaces, open to the sky, can seem threatening, so the best idea is to try and create a room-like space with some sort of enclosure. If there is no low parapet or wall, you will certainly need to put something up anyway, simply from the point of view of safety. The other thing you will find on a roof garden is that the wind is much stronger than at street level and has a dehydrating effect, so plants will need more watering.

✿ You can surround the garden with trellis to act as a psychological barrier and also to help filter the wind to a certain extent. You can plant this quite lightly with ivy or clematis for privacy and leave parts of it unplanted so as not to block the wider view. Choose the most robust trellis you can find and fix it firmly to supports, otherwise the wind will blow it over in a very short time.

may have to have the structure strengthened or you may have to keep pots and plants around the perimeter, close to the structural walls, where the roof is supported.

✿ You must make sure the roof's waterproofing is sound and will not be interfered with. So before you begin, get a structural engineer to check the site for you. In historic or conservation areas, there may be regulations limiting or prohibiting screens or plants being visible from street level, so check with the local authority.

RIGHT: *The first priority for a roof garden is to establish that the roof is strong enough and waterproof and has planning permission for use as a garden. Paving should be as lightweight as possible – thin tiles or decking are probably the best materials. Any pergola should be sturdily fixed to prevent it rocking in the wind and pots should be ranged around the edges of the roof where it is supported.*

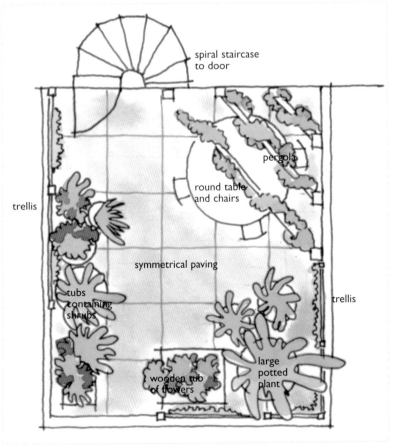

spiral staircase to door

pergola

round table and chairs

trellis

symmetrical paving

tubs containing shrubs

trellis

wooden tub of flowers

large potted plant

## Adding a pergola to a roof

❀ You can add to the enclosed feeling by introducing a small pergola for shade and to support climbers. This will also reduce the effect of the possibly rather oppressive area of sky and provide privacy from nearby roof gardens. It should be attached to walls and sturdily fixed seats and planters to ensure stability.

BELOW: *This attractive, sunny little roof garden is protected from the elements and neighbours by ivy and a small bay tree. Evergreen herbs such as rosemary are brightened up with the reds of geraniums and pinks of sweet peas.*

ABOVE: *The plants in this small roof garden are mostly low growing so as not to suffer from the wind. They include a Mexican orange blossom (Choisya ternata 'Sundance'), some low bamboos, variegated hostas, broom, ceratostigma, lavender and, for climbers, solanum and clematis.*

## Flooring materials

❀ Lightweight gravel is a good foil to small containers. Decking is comparatively lightweight and therefore suitable for a flat roof. Timber tiles are available, which are easy to lay and convenient to carry upstairs. If you have enough space, you can add a raised area of decking to use as a table or for sunbathing.

❀ Roberto Burle Marx, the celebrated Brazilian garden designer, uses brightly coloured mosaic designs as a prominent feature on the floors of his roof gardens and, provided you have a suitable surface, this is an idea that would look cheerful on small roof terraces, too.

## Planters and containers

❀ Most flat roof spaces have some unfortunate built-in features such as a water tank or air-conditioning unit that you cannot get rid of. Portable timber planters of varying heights can be used to hide such eyesores. Fill them with lightweight, moisture retentive compost and plant them up with small trees to make an effective screen. You can paint containers to match any trellis or wall. White is always effective, but there are many excellent colours to choose from and you might prefer a pastel colour or something bolder like a deep blue.

## Plants for the roof

❀ If your roof space is open to the sky, it will probably be best to choose a few carefully placed sculptural plants that will thrive in difficult high-rise urban circumstances, or put containers around the perimeter, planted with wind-resistant shrubs and small trees. Cacti and succulents are sun lovers, and require the minimum of watering. If the temperature is too cold for them, use grasses, which do not need much maintenance and will look very attractive blowing in the wind.

❀ If the space is small and partly enclosed, you could create a bower of flowering shrubs and climbers with a few small conifers for height, variety and shade. Plants that tolerate seaside conditions are often good for rooftop gardens; varieties of *Escallonia*, *Berberis* and *Lauristinus* should all be able to cope with high-rise conditions.

## Balconies

❀ A balcony can become a useful visual and physical extension to the living area. A very effective way of integrating the two areas is to stand a few pots on the inside as well as the outside to act as links and make the balcony seem larger. Use identical pots and flowers to emphasise the sense of unity. If your scheme involves structural work, get advice from a structural engineer as to the weight capacity of your balcony, as you would for a flat roof.

## Window gardens

❀ If window boxes and hanging baskets are the only garden you have, make the most of them. It is wonderful that English pubs have gone so wholeheartedly for

ABOVE: *This large, sunny roof garden has been treated rather formally, with rows of white-flowered geraniums in black pots along the bottom of the window and purple violas climbing up the steps.*

highly coloured hanging baskets and window boxes. Many are truly splendid in their rich and varied plantings, but all the best ones have very deliberate colour schemes. They are not simply a chaos of any old colours planted together.

❀ If you like these cheerful displays, note down what plants have been used to create them and do the same at home. However, not every window box gardener wants to be quite so flamboyant. There are plenty of other ways of making the most of window boxes. The mixed colours of red and white pelargoniums with some trailing ivy will look bright and cheerful all summer.

❀ Herb window boxes can be both charming and useful. Choose herbs that all like the same conditions and that will grow to much the same sort of height or the display won't work or will look unbalanced. Sage, golden marjoram, a dwarf lavender and chives could make an interesting and tasty display.

❀ If the window is on the shady side of the house, you can plant miniature bamboos in window boxes, which will provide a sort of lacy curtain of green. Choose containers that suit the style of the house and make sure the boxes are firmly secured.

# GETTING TO WORK

**Even if you have only a small area of garden, you will want to maximise its potential for privacy and practicality and make it a place in which to relax and enjoy your plants.**

❁

Patio or courtyard gardens look wonderful with a floor of stone or brick paving or wooden decking, and provide a marvellous setting for your plants in containers. This chapter has practical suggestions for all your 'hard surface' needs.

❁

Creating a boundary is also important in a garden, whether for privacy, security, or as a foil for your planting scheme. The fence or wall you erect is going to become a permanent feature, so make sure you choose the most appropriate type for your garden. Whatever type you choose, you can use plants in containers to complement the style of boundary or even to delineate an area of the garden.

❁

And if you plan to spend summer evenings making the most of the garden, a few well-placed lights to highlight your favourite container plants will help create a perfectly cosy outside room.

# BUILDING HARD SURFACES

The garden floor can be a very dominant element in a garden design, yet its planning is all too often neglected in favour of perhaps the more exciting part of gardening – planting. Although most gardeners take great pride in their lawns, which are, essentially, living, green garden floors, the same attention is not lavished on hard-floored areas. An expanse of grey concrete, interrupted only by the odd weed, is not going to enhance any garden. The visual impact of hard flooring, particularly in large-scale applications such as driveways and patios, is often not considered until installation is complete, by which time it is too late to change your mind.

### The planning stage

❀ Take home as many samples of hard flooring as you need, and view them *in situ* for several days before making a decision. Since hard surfaces are a critical part of the permanent structure of a garden design, highly visible even when most of the plants are dormant, you need to choose the material according to the style of your garden and house, as well as for practical and economical reasons.

❀ A path of modern grey slabs will clearly do nothing to enhance a 17th-century red-brick house. Equally, a herringbone path of weathered old paving bricks would look wildly uncomfortable in an austere urban setting.

❀ As well as being a prominent visual feature, hard surfaces are important practical components within the garden. They work hard for their keep, yet are often ignored until problems occur, such as frozen puddles in a pathway which trip up the unwary pedestrian.

ABOVE: *Plan your terracing carefully to maximise sunlight and create different flooring patterns and levels to add interest to the area.*

ABOVE: *Cobbles are uncomfortable to walk on, so stepping stones provide a welcome contrasting surface.*

ABOVE: *Gravel is an inexpensive yet elegant garden flooring material.*

Proper planning at the outset, choosing materials appropriate to the situation and purpose, and simple routine maintenance, will give you a garden floor to be proud of.

❀ The type of material you choose for a path or drive will largely depend on its primary function. For example, a path intended chiefly for decoration, which will barely be walked on, will have quite different demands placed on it than the walkway that leads to your front door.

### Practical matters

❀ Consider whether your preferred material is suitable for the design of your path, drive or other hard surfaced area. For example, gravel or crazy paving can easily be used to make an intricately winding path, but to produce an undulating narrow shape in large paving slabs would involve a lot of tedious calculation and cutting, and would not necessarily look natural or comfortable on completion.

❀ It may sound obvious, but make sure that your hard surfaces are adequately sized for their function. As a rough guide, paths need to be at least 1 m (3 ft) wide to allow comfortable access. Do not assume, if you are replacing an existing hard surface, that you automatically lay a new surface the same size as the old one. It is all too easy to have a driveway or parking space professionally, and expensively, laid only to find that it is too small for your car, or too cramped to allow room for your vehicle and pedestrian access around it.

❀ Mark out your proposed design with rope or a hose, or by dropping dry sand through a funnel to leave a trail. Check out the area from every angle, preferably over a period of a few days. This is especially important in areas like patios, which are garden rooms as well as hard surfaces.

❀ You will want to make sure that the area you are planning to use for entertaining receives the kind of light you want, at the time of day the patio will most commonly be used. For example, if you are installing a patio chiefly for early evening dining, there is no point placing it next to the house if the sunlight is at the other end of your garden at that time.

## TYPES OF HARD SURFACE

THERE are a number of options to choose from, when it comes to creating a hard floor in your garden.

### Bricks

❀ It is tempting to economise on bricks for paving, but the shortcomings of using ordinary house bricks for this demanding function become clear all too quickly. Their porosity means that as water penetrates, freezes, then expands, it cracks away the layers of brick, creating an uneven, flaky, broken surface. This is unsightly and can also be dangerous to walk on, particularly when used as steps.

❀ Engineering bricks are often specified for paving instead, as they are much denser and impervious to water. However, they can become slippery when wet, so 'special' quality bricks are the recommended choice. These are also weather resistant, but are not so prone to weather damage.

❀ Second-hand bricks make a very attractive path, which tones in well with old buildings, but always check that you are buying proper pavers, not simply old house bricks sold as pavers. Insist on a written description if possible. Reliable architectural salvage companies are generally quite happy to provide such a guarantee, since they should be aware of the provenance of the salvaged material.

### Stone

❀ Natural stone, once the first choice in path making, has been superseded in popularity by cast alternatives, due to the high cost of the real thing.

❀ Flagstones of slate, limestone, York stone or sandstone are exceptionally beautiful, as well as hard-wearing, and can be chosen to complement the local stone. Being of natural origin, they also harmonise wonderfully with plant, water and other organic garden elements. Their irregular surface and random patterning can never truly be mimicked by cast alternatives, but the difficulty of cutting them and their expense place them firmly in the luxury bracket.

### Cobblestones

❀ The naturally rounded surface of cobblestones makes them uncomfortable to walk on, so their use is best restricted to ornamental applications. You could break up an expanse of paving slabs by interspersing the slabbed area with areas of cobblestones. They provide an interesting shift in texture, and complement planting well.

❀ Cobbles may be laid loose, or set in concrete or mortar for a more permanent, formal effect. Always ensure that the tops of the stones are level for an even finish for walking on.

### Wood and bark

❀ Natural materials are particularly appropriate and attractive in a woodland, or semi-wild setting, which would look uncomfortable paved with a harsh, non-organic surface such as concrete. Sawn rounds of timber are surprisingly hard-wearing as pavers if they are well treated by soaking in preservative prior to installation, then laid on a bed of sand on top of perforated polythene sheeting.

❀ Fill the gaps between the circles with a sand and gravel mix or chipped bark. Bark needs topping up every few years as it slowly degrades. Wooden decking is getting increasingly popular as exterior flooring, and looks good in urban or country locations. Wooden rounds are also often used as stepping stones across a lawn.

ABOVE: *Decking is a decidedly contemporary flooring material, ideally suited to modern urban gardens.*

## Concrete

❀ Concrete may not be the most attractive hard garden surface, but it is probably the most durable, relatively inexpensive, maintenance free if properly installed and suitable for awkward shapes such as winding paths and driveways.

❀ Essentially, concrete consists of cement combined with an aggregate (fine particles of stone). These dry ingredients are mixed with water, which reacts chemically with the cement and binds the stone particles into a firm, compacted material capable of withstanding tough treatment.

❀ Various mixtures of concrete are used, incorporating, for example, PVA to enhance frost resistance, and/or pigments to produce colours other than the usual grey.

❀ For small jobs, concrete can be mixed by hand, but for more extensive areas, it is well worth hiring a concrete mixer, or having ready-mixed concrete delivered direct to the site. Careful preparation of the site is critical. All too often, concrete is seen as the easy paving option, but if added to an unstable, inadequately prepared surface, the results will be unsatisfactory.

❀ Concrete is also available formed into cast slabs, which can mimic real stone. These provide a popular, affordable alternative to real stone paving.

## Gravel

❀ Gravel is another popular and versatile material. It can withstand heavy use on a driveway, yet is equally suited to small-scale settings such as walkways through a herb garden. Gravel is easy to install, even in curved situations, but for best effect needs to be placed on a proper bed of consolidated coarse gravel.

brick patterns

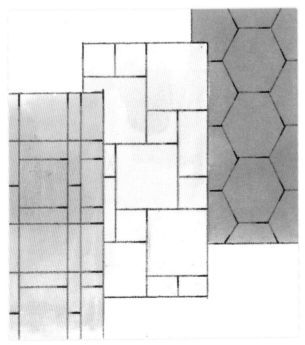

paving slab patterns

decking patterns

## PATIOS

ALTHOUGH, technically, a patio is an area paved with flagstones, enclosed by walls, it has come to be used as a generic term for a hard-surfaced area, usually, but not always, adjoining a house, which is used for relaxing and entertaining. Installing a patio is quite a major undertaking, and needs extremely careful planning and preparation. Mistakes are costly, and permanent.

### Customising an existing patio

❀ You may have inherited a patio that is technically sound, and performs its practical function perfectly, but which is bland and uninspiring. Sympathetic planting can do much to improve matters, without extensive structural work.

❀ Container plants look thoroughly at home on patios, and can be changed seasonally. Choose the style and materials of the containers to link the patio with the house.

❀ Removing some of the slabs and replacing them with planting, and/or other surfaces, such as cobbles, broken slate, gravel or coloured aggregate, will also enliven the overall scheme. You could also introduce vertical elements to break up an overlarge expanse of paving, for example trellis, a pergola, raised beds that incorporate seating, or simply a stunning table, chairs and parasol.

ABOVE: *Although patios were originally made up of stone flags, nowadays more and more people are opting for wooden decking.*

## PLANNING A PATIO

THERE is a surprising amount to think about when planning a patio, if you want to create a feature that will be as visually attractive as it is practical. It is easy to be swayed into buying a load of paving because it appealed on one sunny afternoon in the garden centre, or was on special offer, only to find that it is quite unsuitable when installed.

### Site

❀ Of course, a patio adjoining the house is ideal. Food, drinks, books and cushions may be easily transported between house and garden, particularly if you are fortunate enough to have French doors that lead directly on to the patio.

❀ However, if the area that initially suggests itself as the patio site is very shaded at the time of day that you plan to use it most, you may want to think about having an additional hard-surfaced area elsewhere in the garden. If the problem is one of light shade, caused by overhanging foliage, then the answer may be as simple as pruning back unwanted growth.

❀ If wind is a problem, but the site is otherwise perfect, then consider installing some form of windbreak, for

ABOVE: *This colourful patio appears at first glance to be stone, but it is decking interwoven with blue strips of wood and small clumps of herbs.*

ABOVE: *The word patio is now a generic term for a hard-surfaced area that is used for relaxing and entertaining.*

example a semi-permeable natural screen such as hurdle fencing, bamboo or an interwoven fence. Privacy may also be an important issue, particularly if you plan to sunbathe and relax on your patio, yet your garden is exposed. Again, natural or artificial screens can come into their own here.

### Size

❀ It may sound obvious, but check that the size of patio you are planning is adequate for your needs. If you just want to sit outside and read occasionally, then technically you will need only a quite limited space, but if you enjoy container gardening, you may want to increase the patio to accommodate significant numbers of sizeable plants.

❀ If you plan to cook outside frequently – perhaps on a large gas-fired barbecue or outdoor stove – and entertain on a regular basis, your requirements will be quite different. You will need space for a table and chairs that will comfortably accommodate your guests, together with space for food cooking and preparation.

### Patio surfaces

❀ Once you have established what the patio is mostly going to be used for, where it is going to be, and how big it needs to be, you can at last turn your attention to how it is going to look. The general guidelines on the previous pages on choosing materials still apply.

❀ Choose a surface to suit your home. Patios are a dominant visual feature, and can just as easily detract from the beauty and value of your home as they can add to it. Do not be tempted to mix too many types of surface in an effort to add interest. By the time a patio has dining seats, sun loungers, perhaps more than one table, possibly lighting, screening, maybe a water feature, together with a barbecue and all the other paraphernalia that tends to accumulate on a patio, it will quickly become very busy looking and is unlikely to need much in the way of added interest underfoot.

❀ Two surfaces are probably the most you will need to create a dynamic, but balanced and restrained patio, for example slabs interspersed with pebbles and planting, or wooden decking bordered by gravel.

## PATHS

Paths are hard-working surfaces. They carry not only foot traffic, but often wheelbarrows, heavily loaded sack trolleys and bicycles, too. They may also be required to permit the regular use of wheelchairs or a pram. If planning a garden from scratch, these individual needs can be catered for.

### Choosing a path

❀ Always make the path sufficiently wide for its purpose. Ideally, two people should be able to walk along a path, side by side, without any sense of being cramped.

❀ Choose materials suited to the surroundings, as well as to the practical requirements placed on them. For example, a tarmac path may be inexpensive and hard-wearing, but will be an unforgiving feature leading up to your front door. It may be worth investing in a more attractive surface for such a prominent position.

### Gravel paths

❀ Washed gravel is an attractive and inexpensive paving material. The ideal size of stone is approximately 2 cm ($^3/_4$ in) in diameter. This generally presents the least problems in terms of stones being brought into the house via shoes.

ABOVE: *Paths should always be planned according to individual requirements; consider what your needs are before deciding on the style of walkway that would suit you best.*

ABOVE: *Here the blue of the sea and gentle pink of the flowers in the background are reflected in the soft colours of the paving on the terrace.*

### Brick paths

❀ Brick paths are particularly attractive and, if created using bricks sympathetic to those used for the house, provide a strong yet unobtrusive visual link between the house and garden. They may be laid in a variety of patterns, including straight or angled herringbone, basket weave and stretcher bond.

### Concrete paving

❀ Concrete is an enduringly popular choice for paving. It is relatively inexpensive, yet very durable. Concrete is only hard-wearing if it is installed properly, so careful planning is essential before starting to prepare the path.

❀ Concrete is a much maligned surface, decried for its bland grey appearance. However, a well-laid concrete path can, in some cases, be more attractive than a more showy surface of ill-proportioned, poorly installed, over-bright imitation stone slabs, which may have cost much more.

### Textural possibilities

❀ You can vary the surface texture of a finished concrete path for added visual interest. The natural surface that results from the tamping process, which completes the path laying, is practical and non-slip, with a slightly rough texture.

❀ The setting concrete may be dragged with a broom to create a subtly striped, rippled finish, or swept with a wooden float for a smooth finish that works well in stark, modern settings. Another option is to mimic the effects of crazy paving by marking the surface of the concrete with a stick to resemble irregularly shaped slabs.

✿ Embedding a decorative aggregate in the surface of the concrete is another option. Scatter dampened pebbles on to the newly laid concrete and tamp with timber until flush with the surface. When all surface water has evaporated, gently wash away cement from around the pebbles until they protrude. An alternative textural finish is achieved by simply washing away the fine surface of the setting concrete to reveal the gravel below.

## LAYING A BRICK PATH

Brick paths need to be laid on a 7.5 cm (3 in) thick, compacted hard core base, topped with a 5 cm (2 in) thick layer of sharp sand.

**1** *Support the bricks with a permanent edging such as timber or a row of bricks set on end into concrete.*

**2** *Set the bricks with fine sand and water well. Ensure that the sand packs down between the bricks. Repeat until the cracks are packed.*

## LAYING A GRAVEL PATH

Prepare a site for gravel well. Edging, to contain the gravel, is very important. Bricks laid on their edge and set in concrete are popular edgings.

**1** *Thoroughly compact the hard core surface for the path, then top it with a 5 cm (2 in) deep layer of coarse gravel.*

**2** *Follow this with a layer of hoggin (clay binder), spread it to fill any cracks, then roll it. Finally, add a 2.5–4 cm (1–1½ in) layer of washed gravel and roll this, too.*

## LAYING CONCRETE PAVING SLABS

Paving slabs are widely available. Choose a finish sympathetic to your garden style for best results. Laying heavy slabs is simple but hard work.

**1** *Take care to set out the slabs and lay them properly for best results. Try to use only whole slabs to avoid the need for cutting slabs.*

**2** *Lay paving slabs on a firm, level base of hard-core topped with sharp sand and tamp them down. A slight, even slope will be needed to allow water to run off the surface. Paint with mortar after a couple of days.*

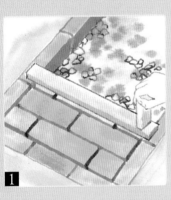

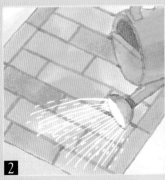

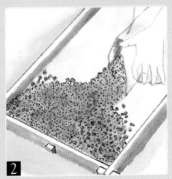

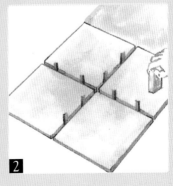

## DRIVEWAYS

DRIVEWAYS have the toughest hard-surface job of all. They need to be able to withstand heavy, continual traffic. Gravel is an attractive, relatively inexpensive material for driveways and makes a satisfying crunch as you park. Concrete is a popular alternative. Commercial contractors can install concrete drives imprinted with patterns. These can be more attractive than flat concrete drives, yet less expensive than specialist individual bricks or slabs.

### Planning driveways

❀ It may sound obvious that the first step in planning a driveway or car parking pad is to ascertain how big the area needs to be, yet it is alarmingly easy to underestimate the amount of space that a vehicle occupies. As a general rule, a minimum width of 3 m (10 ft) is required, but this will vary according to your individual needs – you may regularly need to park a much larger vehicle in your garden. Consider, too, the turning circle of your vehicle.

❀ You may not have unlimited space for a drive, but if you do have a little more than the bare minimum available to give over to a drive, life will be very much more convenient for you. Imagine not having to shout at your children about banging the car doors against the wall or fence on a daily basis, and you might resent less having to give over a little of your garden to the car.

❀ A very easy mistake to make is to forget to allow for opening the car doors, which becomes a real problem if the driveway is close to a wall. Ideally, also allow plenty of space for pedestrian access around parked cars. If you know that prams and bikes are going to be wheeled past your parked car regularly, it is well worth incorporating a little extra space into your driveway to avoid frayed tempers as the paint gets repeatedly

ABOVE: *Be prepared to cut back on your borders to allow space for your parking area.*

scraped away from the side of the car by an exuberant young cyclist.

❀ It is tempting to make driveways as small as possible, since they are not generally things of inherent loveliness. However, if you refuse to move your flowerbed a single inch to accommodate a reasonably sized driveway, you may find your precious perennials destroyed anyway, as people scramble out of the car and across the ornamental borders.

RIGHT: *A hard-working driveway is softened visually by a curved edge and planted border.*

## The importance of slope

❀ Parking areas and driveways must have a sufficient slope to allow water to fall away, so that the surface retains enough traction for vehicles in icy conditions. You do not want puddles forming in the drive, so the surface needs to be absolutely even. When a concrete parking area is laid next to a house, it must slope away markedly from the building, and must be at least 15 cm (6 in) below the damp course.

❀ As a general guide to the degree of fall-off required, a drive needs a 1-in-40 gradient – 2.5 cm per metre (1 in per yard) to be effective. A hard surface such as a parking area or patio installed next to a house needs a 1-in-60 gradient – 1.6 cm per metre ($^5/_8$ in per yard).

## PREVENTING CONCRETE FROM CRACKING

TEMPERATURE changes cause concrete to expand and contract. If this motion is allowed to continue randomly, the surface will crack open at its weakest point. Control joints, also known as expansion joints, made of compressible material such as wooden planks, are added at regular intervals to concentrate or absorb the force of the contraction and expansion.

Pathways need control joints at approximately 2-m (7-ft) intervals, while driveways need such joints every 4 m (13 ft). If a parking area is more than twice as long as its width, or its length is more than 40 times its thickness, you will need to divide the concrete into equal sections with control joints. Control joints are also always needed between concrete that adjoins a wall, and where concrete surrounds inspection chambers.

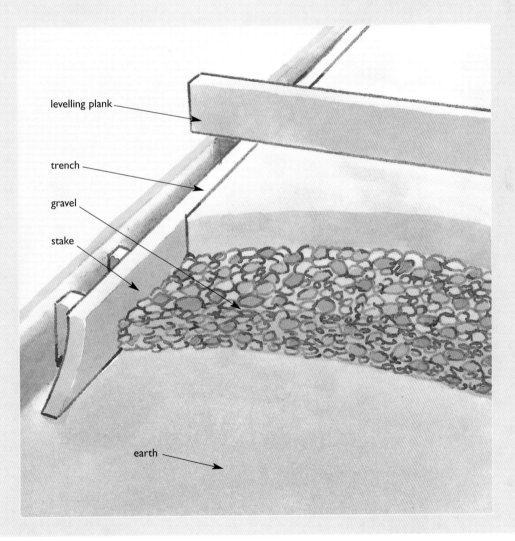

levelling plank

trench

gravel

stake

earth

# GARDEN LIGHTING

❦

In recent years the garden has increasingly come to be regarded as an additional living area, rather than an area purely for planting. Lighting may be purely functional or more atmospheric. It can extend the amount of time you are able to spend in the garden, as well as enhance your view of the garden from the house at night and when the weather is less kind. Garden centres and do-it-yourself (DIY) stores have increased the range of garden lighting available, so a beautifully lit garden is no longer the exclusive preserve of the garden designer.

### Lighting for safety

❀ The first lighting consideration in most gardens is a practical one. At night you should be able to see your way clearly from the garden entrance to your front door. If there are any steps that are difficult to navigate safely in the dark, good lighting will greatly reduce the risk of accidents.

BELOW: *It is important to ensure that areas such as steps, which are difficult to navigate, are well-lit at night.*

❀However, do not install intense, isolated lights, such as spotlights, at potential accident spots. As you move from an area of bright light into sudden darkness, your eyes cannot make the adjustment quickly enough to be safe, and you may have unwittingly increased your chances of a fall. Such areas need a broad spread of light so that the whole journey may be made in the same lighting condition. These lights are sometimes called spread lights.

## Lighting for increased security

❀ Strong illumination around the home is a proven deterrent to intruders. Floodlights with in-built passive infra-red detectors (PIRs) are widely available. Activated by localised changes in heat, these are automatically switched on when a person or animal approaches.

❀ Think carefully about where you place these lights. Although they are undoubtedly effective close to the door, it can be very irritating for both you and your neighbours if the light is placed so that it is constantly being activated by passers-by. Moving the light just a few feet to one side may mean that you will still be able to see clearly to get your key in the door, and would-be intruders are effectively deterred.

❀ PIR lights are available in many styles, so choose one that fits in with the mood of your home. A high-tech light, for example, would look very incongruous outside a Victorian cottage, where a carriage lamp might sit very happily.

BELOW: *Lighting increases the amount of time you can comfortably spend in your garden.*

## Lighting to extend garden use

❀ Al fresco cooking and eating have enjoyed a massive increase in popularity in recent years. Improvements in outdoor cooking methods, such as gas-fired barbecues and even outdoor Mexican-style ovens, have truly turned the garden into an additional room.

❀ When daylight hours grow shorter, there is no need to curtail the pleasures of patio living. Provide adequate light so that cooking and food preparation can continue comfortably, and you will find that outdoor entertaining can start earlier in the year and continue well into the autumn.

❀ Although a simple floodlight fitted to the wall of the house will illuminate a wide area, the light given is not intimate or attractive. More appropriate would be specific lighting of the cooking and eating area, together with lighting to highlight particular points of visual interest around the garden. This may be as simple as a spotlight above the barbecue and lanterns around the table, or a more sophisticated arrangement of permanent lighting throughout the garden.

BELOW: *Effective lighting extends the living space of your home out into the garden.*

## Lighting for effect

❀ Anyone who has gazed out at the garden when it is illuminated for Christmas, even if the lighting is limited to a few fairy lights strung through a lone tree, will appreciate that lighting can increase your enjoyment of the garden, even when you are inside your home. This lighting for added mood is not the same as functional lighting.

❀ An even wash of light over the whole garden will add nothing in terms of charm or romance. Mood lighting, as in the home, comes from distinctly separate areas of light, positioned carefully so as to illuminate features of particular interest. Less attractive features can be left darkened to recede into the shadows.

❀ Just as too many decorative features in a garden can fight for attention and give an overbusy, cluttered look, care should be taken when planning accent lighting. Too many, different types of light can give a disjointed appearance – more appropriate in a large-scale municipal park than in the smaller domestic garden.

❀ A single, silhouetted tree or pond with submerged lights may be all that is required to make an impact. Clear white light is generally best for retaining a naturalistic feel. Reserve coloured lights for special occasions, or you may end up with a garden that looks uncomfortably like a fairy grotto instead of a sophisticated idyll.

*BELOW: Mains lighting can be expensive and disruptive to install but the results will be worth the effort and expense involved.*

## The practicalities

❀ Most garden lighting will necessitate installation of electricity. There are two types of electric lighting used in the garden – low voltage and mains.

❀ Mains lighting is best considered at the planning stage of a garden, since the cables will need to be laid professionally, at least 46 cm (18 in) underground. This is obviously expensive and disruptive, but is necessary if you want powerful lighting around the garden, if long runs of cable and prolonged lamp life are required, or if you have a broad landscape to illuminate.

❀ Low-voltage lights use a transformer to reduce the voltage, effectively reducing the illumination power available, but also making the lights safer. The main advantage of a low-voltage system is that there is no need to submerge the cables.

❀ Heavy-duty low-voltage cable can even run along the soil surface if necessary, although it is better to submerge cable if possible, and house it in protective conduit to avoid damage while cultivating the garden.

*BELOW: Subtle recessed lights are useful for unobtrusive illumination of areas such as walkways and steps.*

## Lighting patterns

❀ Generally, lighting falls into two categories –
spotlighting and floodlighting. The difference is in
the spread of light. Spotlighting is a narrow beam
with sharp definition at the edges of the beam;
floodlighting is a wide beam falling off softly at the
edges. Either type may be used to create different
effects, such as uplighting, backlighting and
downlighting, although spotlighting is most often
used because of its controlled, narrow beam.

❀ Backlighting is created by placing light behind
a feature, for example a statue, so that it is thrown
into dramatic silhouette. Uplighting entails placing
light at ground level, pointing up at a plant or other
feature. Mature trees look particularly striking lit
in this way.

❀ Downlighting is self-explanatory – literally a light
pointing downwards. This can be functional, such
as wall lights pointing towards the patio, or used for
dramatic effect, as in moonlighting, where lights are
placed in a tree pointing downwards to imitate
moonlight. Just as soft pools of downlight from table
lamps create intimacy in the home, downlighting in
the garden gives a cosy feel.

## Types of external lights

❀ Most people will be familiar with wall-mounted
external lights, such as those used to illuminate the
front door or the area around garages and sheds. Post
lights are also popular. In addition to the familiar
carriage lamp-style post lights, there are shorter post
lights available. These have a smaller spread of light
and are a more subtle alternative.

❀ Spike lights may be less familiar, but are well worth
exploring for their flexibility of use. This type of light
is pushed into the lawn or soil, and is available both as
a fixed position light, or one with an adjustable angle,
so that specific lighting effects can be achieved.

❀ Recessed lights, such as those that replace bricks in
walls bordering paths, can be very useful for lighting
walkways safely yet unobtrusively. Whatever the
choice, it is important not to get carried away with the
exciting possibilities of garden lighting. The aim
should be to enhance the garden with lighting, not
dominate it.

RIGHT: *These garden steps are lit by an unusual and attractive lamp.*

# ESTABLISHING BOUNDARIES

Boundaries are an important consideration in garden planning.
Not only do they mark the limitations of your property, they also provide
the opportunity to screen out noise and unsightly views and
to afford privacy. Conversely, your garden may enjoy a wonderful
view and have no issues of privacy or noise pollution. Thus, marking
the boundary may consist of a visually minimal delineation, such as
installing a chain-link fence. Within the garden itself, fences,
walls and screens, such as a collection of plants in containers,
offer a way of marking out distinct zones of activity, such as
play areas and vegetable plots, as well as providing vertical surfaces
for planting and concealing ugly but necessary parts of the garden,
such as compost bins and recycling areas.

## BOUNDARY TYPES

THE issues to consider when choosing a type of boundary are straightforward, and governed by common sense as well as visual preference.

### Tall, solid boundaries

❀ If you need to enhance the level of privacy in your garden, you will be considering solid, tall options, such as high walls or closeboard fencing. Walls will block out noise, as well as prying eyes, better than fences. In

both cases, remember that tall, solid screens also block out light and can seem claustrophobic in small areas, so plan carefully before purchasing and installing.

❀ There may also be local, as well as national, planning restrictions on the type and height of boundary marking that may be placed on your property, so do research any such limitations at the outset.

❀ A final point of consideration is that, contrary to popular belief, a solid wall or fence does not offer the best protection on an exposed site, and can even lead to problems such as the creation of a plant-damaging frost pocket, instability of the barrier itself, and turbulent, plant-harming wind conditions on either side of the barrier.

### Partially open boundaries

❀ Where a solid wall or fence would be inappropriate, a partially occluded screen may be the answer. For example, a wattle fence appears almost solid but actually allows some air to penetrate, and so makes an effective windbreak in exposed situations where an impenetrable barrier would cause problems.

❀ Certain types of partially open boundaries also offer a degree of privacy and security, while allowing some light to pass through them, for example walls topped with screen blocks, or fences headed with decorative trellis.

LEFT: *A partially occluded screen such as a decorative trellis can be used to create a boundary without building a solid wall or fence, and serves as a decorative feature as well as creating a feeling of space.*

ABOVE: *Fencing materials define the borders of a plot and need to be sympathetic to the overall theme of the garden, such as this bamboo, used to reinforce a Japanese style.*

## Open boundaries

❀ Some boundary markings are just that – a way of delineating the extremities of your property, without affording marked additional degrees of privacy, sound reduction or security. There are various options available, some more decorative and practically useful than others.

❀ Prices also vary widely. For example, a cast-iron fence can be highly ornamental and offers some security enhancement if it is sufficiently tall and of an intricate and pointed design that is off-putting to the casual fence-climbing intruder. Such fences can be expensive and will need ongoing maintenance in order to retain its elegant good looks, whether purchased new or from a specialist in architectural salvage.

RIGHT: *A tall, solid boundary such as closeboard fencing can be used to enhance the privacy of your garden, but remember that it will also block out light.*

## WALLS

WALLS are more permanent structures than fences and, correspondingly, need thorough planning before building begins. They are very effective at noise reduction, and of course offer maximum privacy. High walls may seem to offer an increased level of security, since it is obviously more difficult to climb over a wall than to step over a chain-link fence. Bear in mind, however, that an intruder can work unseen and unheard behind the useful concealment of a high wall, so a lower wall may be a better option where security is a more important consideration than privacy.

### Choosing a wall

❀ Walls are generally made of brick, concrete or stone, and may be solid or pierced, as in the case of a wall made of screen blocks. Always choose materials that are sympathetic to those used in the construction of your home, and appropriate to the style of wall prevalent in your area.

❀ For example, an old cottage built of stone would look very uncomfortable surrounded by a wall of concrete blocks. Similarly, a stark, modern home would look very awkward partnered by an overly rustic dry stone wall. Observe the materials and styles used in other gardens around your own, and make a note of what works and what is less successful.

## BRICKS

❀ Clay bricks are attractive, and are available in a wide variety of colours, textures and degrees of weather resistance. Ordinary facing bricks are fine for most garden walls, but 'special' quality bricks will be required for applications where increased water resistance is needed, such as on exposed walls in coastal regions.

❀ Salvaged bricks are not necessarily a cheaper option than new bricks, but may be the best choice for producing a wall that tones in well with the brickwork of your home.

ABOVE: *Walls can be prettified considerably with planting. Here, the fan-trained pears are attractive as well as productive.*

ABOVE: *The severity of a solid brick wall is softened by a round window and arched doorway.*

❀ If you have any spare house bricks available to take to the builder's merchant for matching, so much the better. Always obtain a sample to take home to assess whether the tone, texture and colouring really work well *in situ*. Building a wall is a costly investment in terms of time and money, and mistakes are all too glaringly obvious when replicated in row after row of inappropriate brick.

## BLOCKS

❀ Blocks are obviously quicker to lay than bricks, since they are so much larger. However, the foundations of a block wall are just as important, so do not regard building a block wall as any less serious an undertaking as laying a brick wall.

❀ The all-too-common garden sight of a shoddily built collapsing concrete wall bears testimony to the fact that block walling is seen by many people as a speedy and inexpensive alternative.

### Natural blocks

❀ Stone walling is very attractive, and indigenous to some areas. Indeed, some districts even have planning regulations that necessitate the use of local stone for new walls. Granite, limestone and sandstone are all used for wall building. Flint and slate are also used, often in combination with other materials.

❀ It makes economic sense to buy from a local quarry or salvage company. Garden centres often have a selection of appealing stone, but to buy there the sort of quantities needed for a run of walling, rather than isolated pieces for a small rockery, would be prohibitively expensive.

### Concrete blocks

❀ Standard structural blocks are inexpensive and easy to lay, although they are not attractive and their use is generally limited to areas where they will be later disguised by a coat of rendering or plastering. A zigzag pattern on their surface provides a key to encourage adhesion of these materials.

❀ Facing blocks have a decorative face and end, and are used for the external surface of cavity walls, backed by plain, structural blocks. They are available in a wide range of finishes to tone in with local stone, are cheaper than reconstituted stone blocks or natural stone, but much less visually convincing than either.

❀ Reconstituted stone blocks use crushed stone in place of aggregate, and are moulded into a range of shapes from smooth to rough hewn, and in colours to suit most local stone types. Although more realistic than facing blocks, they do not have the same lack of uniformity that characterises natural stone.

❀ Screen blocks are concrete blocks pierced with a decorative pattern, and are generally used to form walls produced in a stack-bonded pattern – literally piled up in columns rather than being offset. This produces a weaker wall than traditional bond patterns, so screen walls need supporting piers at each end for additional strength.

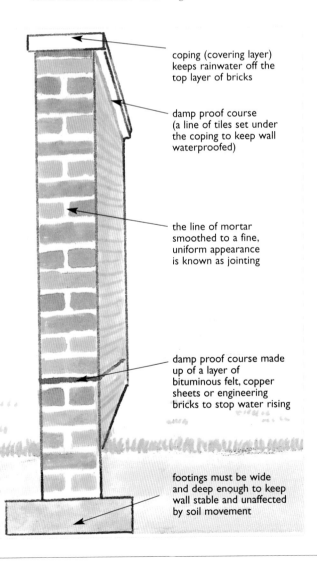

coping (covering layer) keeps rainwater off the top layer of bricks

damp proof course (a line of tiles set under the coping to keep wall waterproofed)

the line of mortar smoothed to a fine, uniform appearance is known as jointing

damp proof course made up of a layer of bituminous felt, copper sheets or engineering bricks to stop water rising

footings must be wide and deep enough to keep wall stable and unaffected by soil movement

## TYPES OF FENCE

Fences come in a wide range of styles and use a variety of materials, namely wire, concrete, plastic and timber. Forms of fencing available include such options as two or three lengths of sturdy wire threaded through upright posts, chain link fencing and ready-made wooden panels, among many others; and prices vary considerably, according to the type of fence chosen.

### Post and chain fencing

❀ Post and chain fencing marks a boundary and deters people from straying from a path on to a lawn or flowerbed, but affords no additional privacy or enhanced security.

❀ Lengths of metal or plastic chain, which are available in several link types and colours, are suspended between wooden or metal posts. The most commonly used arrangement is a black-painted metal chain of oval links, alternating with diamond spikes, hung from white-painted posts.

### Trellis fencing

❀ Trellis fencing has become increasingly popular in recent years. Used to divide the garden into separate areas, conceal unsightly views or top a solid fence, trellis is comparatively inexpensive, easy to install, wonderfully compatible with planting and suitable for many situations, since it allows light and air to pass freely through it.

❀ Trellis comes in many styles, sizes and variants – from rustic larch poles, which give a quaint, country cottage feel, to sophisticated shapes in smooth wood.

❀ The method of installing trellis will depend on the type used. Insubstantial concertina-fold trellis needs to be housed in a stout holding frame for added stability, whereas split larch poles, nailed on to sturdy posts and rails properly installed in the ground, produces a stable and attractive fence.

### Closeboard fencing

❀ Closeboard fencing consists of vertically overlapped wooden featherboard strips, nailed on to horizontal rails. Cedar is the best quality wood for this, and is correspondingly expensive. Softwood is the more affordable option.

❀ Both types are attractive and strong and provide a high degree of privacy. Because the strips are vertical, the fence is not easy to climb, deterring children from attempting to scale it. Closeboard fencing is a good but expensive option for adding privacy to a sloping garden. It can be erected *in situ* – or made from 'off-the-peg' panels.

### Picket fencing

❀ Picket, or palisade fencing, particularly when painted white, immediately conjures up images of country cottages and old-fashioned charm.

❀ Narrow vertical pales are spaced approximately 5 cm (2 in) apart, attached to horizontal rails. The tops of the pales may be pointed, rounded, or cut into decorative shapes such as Gothic-style finials. This fencing is highly decorative and is used primarily as an ornamental way of marking a boundary rather than to provide privacy, since it is open, and is also usually no more than 1.2 m (4 ft) high.

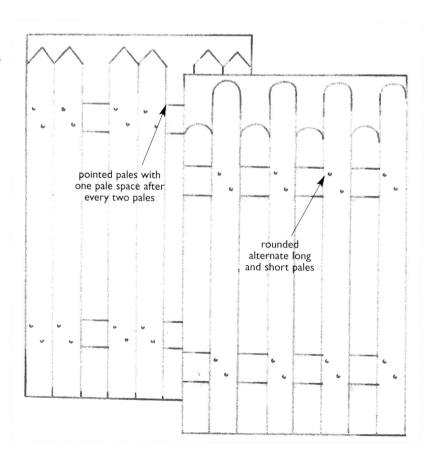

pointed pales with one pale space after every two pales

rounded alternate long and short pales

## Ranch-style fencing

❀ As its name suggests, ranch-style fencing brings to mind the wide open spaces of the American plains. It is simply constructed from wide horizontal rails attached to stout boards. Made in soft- or hardwood, it may be painted or simply treated with weatherproofing.

❀ Low-maintenance plastic ranch-style fencing is also available. Removed from a large-scale, ranch-style context of bordering a field, this type of fencing can look somewhat oversized and municipal, and affords no privacy.

❀ This style of fencing is also irresistible to children as a ready made climbing frame and to passing adults as a convenient leaning post and makeshift seat; these are points worth considering if your boundary lies next to a bus stop or telephone box. Finding that you have spent a considerable amount of time and money in installing what is in effect a public bench could prove very irritating.

## ANATOMY OF A FENCE

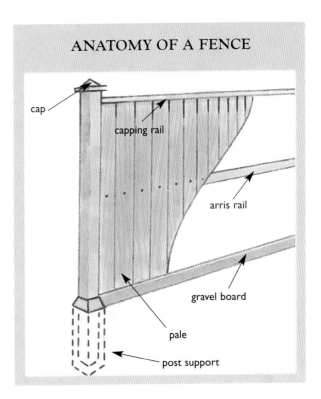

cap

capping rail

arris rail

gravel board

pale

post support

## BUILDING A PICKET FENCE

*Fence posts must be extremely sturdy and firmly positioned when constructing a fence.*

**1** *Sink each post at least 60 cm (24 in) into the ground for good stability. Metal post spikes remove the need for digging and concreting as they are simply hammered into position, but are suitable only for firm ground. If you are not using metal spikes, you will need* to dig a hole, fill the bottom with compacted hard core, then concrete the fence post in place. Chamfer off the concrete just above ground level.

**2** *Fix the arris rails to the fence posts. Fix the pickets to* the arris rails, taking care to place them evenly.

**3** *Use a picket to act as a spacing guide. Keep the top of the pickets level by working to a string line suspended between the fence posts.*

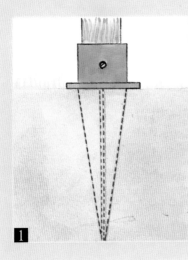

## PANEL FENCES

FENCES made from ready-made panels nailed between wooden posts are popular because they offer a reasonable level of privacy at relatively little expense, and are quite simple to erect. Various types are available.

### Interwoven panels

❀ These are made of thin wooden strips woven between vertical stiffeners to produce a closed, but not totally occlusive fence. Choose good-quality interwoven panels with strips that fit tightly against each other, since the wood may shrink back in the summer and leave unsightly gaps.

### Hurdle fencing

❀ Hurdle fencing is another type of interwoven panel, made from strips of flexible branches such as willow woven horizontally around sturdy upright wooden poles. It is an effective windbreak, since some air is allowed to pass through it.

❀ Hurdle fencing has become increasingly popular in garden design because it gives instant rustic appeal at comparatively low cost, and is made from natural materials from renewable sources.

ABOVE: *Ready-made panel fences are a popular choice, since they are reasonably cheap to buy and easy to erect.*

❀ Although not as permanent an investment as a brick wall or closeboard fence, hurdle panels will last for several years, and make very pretty garden screening. Short hurdle fences are perfect for edging borders, and can be made *in situ* or bought ready-made.

### Horizontally lapped panels

❀ Slightly more expensive than interwoven panels, these are more durable and offer greater privacy, since there are no gaps for prying eyes to peep through. Strips of wood, usually larch, are overlapped horizontally, and held between a sawn timber frame.

❀ The strips may have a smooth, straight edge or, for a more informal feel, are available with undulating edges with or without the bark attached.

### Vertically lapped panels

❀ Self-descriptive, these panels of overlapping vertical strips, attached to a frame, make a durable, peep-proof fence, which mimics closeboard fencing. Choose good-quality panels that are well overlapped so that gaps do not appear as the wood shrinks with changing weather conditions.

### Interlap fencing

❀ Interlap fencing consists of square-edged boards nailed to horizontal rails, and fixed on alternating sides. It is a popular choice for an exposed site, as it is sturdy, yet wind is allowed to pass through the gaps between the boards.

LEFT: *The appearance of panel fencing is greatly improved by sympathetic planting.*

❀ Where wind is not a problem the boards may be spaced as you wish – overlapped for more privacy, or spaced more widely to allow light to pass through. The construction method means that interlap fencing is equally attractive on both sides – another reason for its popularity.

### Chestnut palings

❀ Sold by the roll, this consists of a series of parallel chestnut stakes, fixed together top and bottom with lengths of twisted wire to form a cheap fence.

❀ Attached to sturdy posts at 1.8 m (6 ft) intervals, chestnut palings produce an effective barrier, but do not offer increased privacy. Although not particularly attractive, this type of fencing is light, easy to transport and install, and blends quiet inconspicuously into its surroundings, especially if softened by planting.

### Post and wire fencing

❀ Post and wire fencing comprises two or three lengths of sturdy wire stretched between strong posts of wood, concrete or steel and kept taut by straining bolts.

❀ The posts must be firmly fixed and well supported. The end posts will need supportive struts. Although privacy and security are not improved by this type of fence, it is an inexpensive, unobtrusive way of marking a boundary while a hedge is growing, as it also offers good support for the hedge itself.

### Chain link fencing

❀ Chain link fencing comprises plastic-coated or galvanised wire mesh, attached to firm posts of wood or concrete. Choose a mesh colour that tones in with its surroundings.

❀ This fence type is familiar in municipal settings. Not the most attractive boundary option, it does offer optimum light transmission, some measure of additional security and is comparatively cheap and easy to install.

### Wire picket fencing

❀ Plastic-coated wire hoops are linked together and fixed on to posts to make a discreet fence, which does not improve security or privacy but is a popular, inexpensive way of marking out boundaries and, in particular, flower borders and beds.

❀ The posts need to be sturdy and well fixed, and the wire panel held taut between them. Miniature versions are available for edging borders and paths at ankle height.

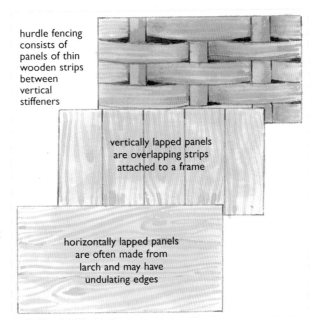

hurdle fencing consists of panels of thin wooden strips between vertical stiffeners

vertically lapped panels are overlapping strips attached to a frame

horizontally lapped panels are often made from larch and may have undulating edges

### Concrete fencing

❀ This fence is a popular choice in municipal applications, valued for its minimal maintenance requirements and ease of installation compared with a brick wall.

❀ Slabs of interlocking concrete are slid horizontally between grooves in pre-formed concrete posts to make a solid, masonry wall that does not need foundations as brick walls do. It is difficult to climb, so enhances security, but blocks out light, is brutally unattractive and is also quite expensive.

BELOW: *A white painted heavy wooden wall can reflect the light in strong sunshine.*

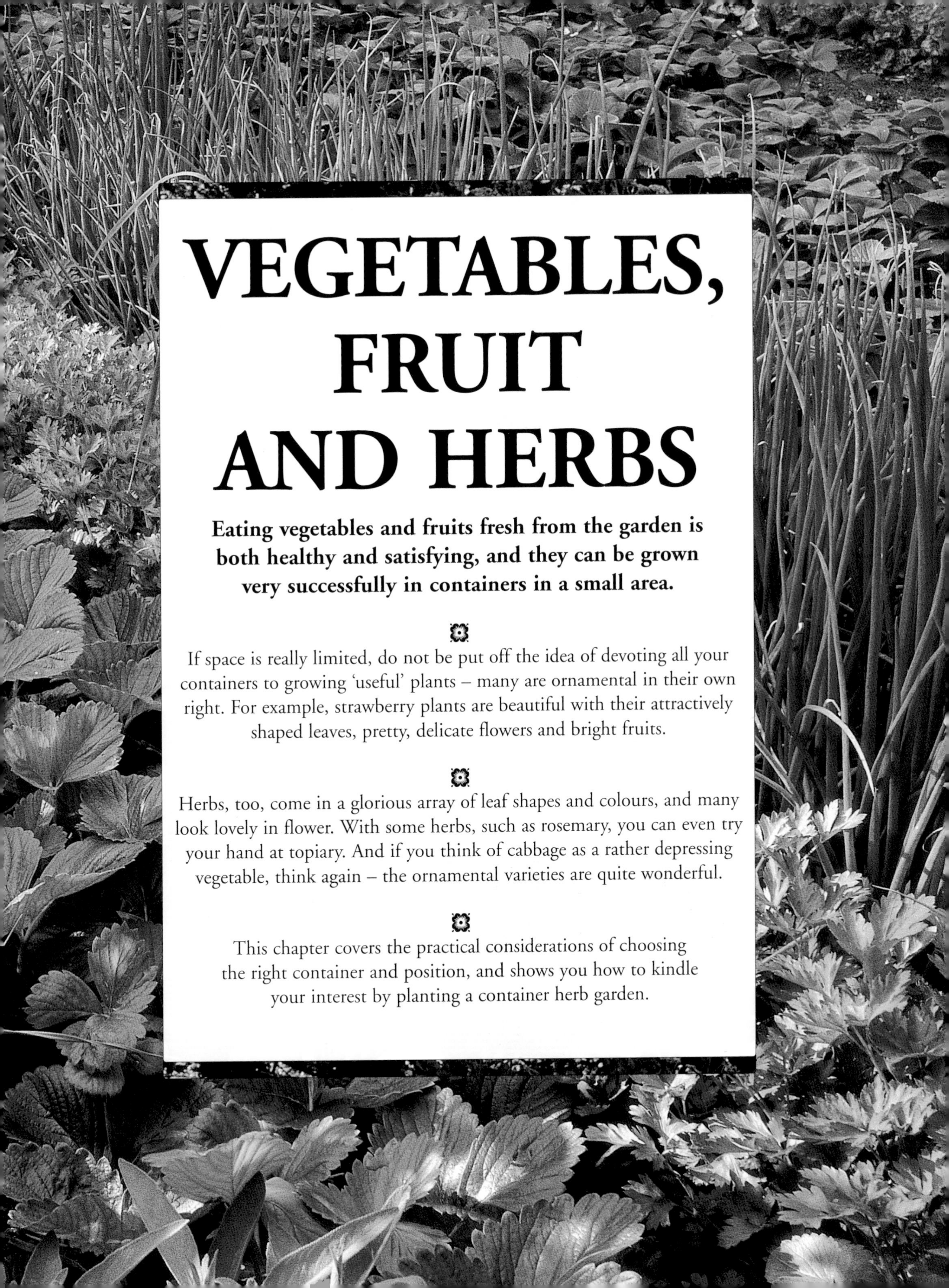

# VEGETABLES, FRUIT AND HERBS

**Eating vegetables and fruits fresh from the garden is both healthy and satisfying, and they can be grown very successfully in containers in a small area.**

✿

If space is really limited, do not be put off the idea of devoting all your containers to growing 'useful' plants – many are ornamental in their own right. For example, strawberry plants are beautiful with their attractively shaped leaves, pretty, delicate flowers and bright fruits.

✿

Herbs, too, come in a glorious array of leaf shapes and colours, and many look lovely in flower. With some herbs, such as rosemary, you can even try your hand at topiary. And if you think of cabbage as a rather depressing vegetable, think again – the ornamental varieties are quite wonderful.

✿

This chapter covers the practical considerations of choosing the right container and position, and shows you how to kindle your interest by planting a container herb garden.

ABOVE: *Raised beds ease the work of the vegetable gardener and look neat and attractive.*

## VEGETABLES IN CONTAINERS

GROWING vegetables in containers has developed from the ubiquitous commercial growing bag of tomatoes that starts many gardeners on the path towards more ambitious vegetable gardening. Even gardeners with extremely limited space to devote to vegetables are able to produce edible crops, which not only taste great, are chemical free, vitamin rich and super fresh, but also attractive plants in their own right. Cabbages, for example, are increasingly grown not only as food crops, but for their ornamental properties. There are breeds of tomato that have a delightful tumbling growth habit, perfectly suited to containers such as hanging baskets and the multi-holed terracotta pots, more usually seen housing strawberries.

❀ Growing vegetables in containers has many other benefits besides maximising space. The soil pest problems, weeding and digging that make vegetable growing in open soil hard work are eradicated. Since container-grown vegetables are portable, you can grow plants that need particular local environments, moving them as necessary to suit the changing climate and their individual needs.

❀ For example, you may be able to grow tender vegetables, which need a sheltered spot, against a sunny wall, far away from the main, exposed vegetable plot where they would perish. Choose containers sufficiently sized to suit the crop. For example, long-rooted vegetables such as carrots need a depth of at least 46 cm (18 in) to flourish, while a lettuce can thrive in a window box.

### DRAWBACKS

A disadvantage of container growing vegetables is that you will need to pay particular attention to watering and feeding. Another issue to consider is that plastic growing bags are not attractive, and can be quite unsightly if you have a lot of them, undisguised, surrounding your house.

## THE ORNAMENTAL POTAGER

PLANNING a vegetable garden that is ornamental as well as productive has become very fashionable. Potager is the French word for kitchen garden, but is now used internationally to describe a garden where edible plants are grown with an emphasis on their decorative potential. Other elements are included to produce an area that is as pretty as it is productive – for example neat pathways of brick or gravel passing between geometric beds enclosed by formal dwarf box hedging, sometimes embellished further with vines, roses and grapes draped over arches traversing the walkways.

❀ Many of the vegetables in the potager are chosen for their visual appeal, for example leaf beet and red lettuces, although even ordinary varieties appear more attractive when displayed in such a charming setting.

## VEGETABLES IN THE BORDER

INCORPORATING vegetables within the herbaceous border has also become increasingly acceptable and fashionable. Many gardeners do not have the space to devote a whole area to vegetables, along with the attendant demands on time and the potential production of crop gluts, which can be difficult to handle without wastage.

❀ Gardeners have mixed flowers with edible crops for many years, although historically, cottage gardeners would have been concerned with having herbs to hand for practical reasons, and any decorative effect would have been fairly incidental.

❀ Today, ornamental crops, as in the potager, are often selected in preference to more workaday species. For example, ruby chard, a variety of leaf beet, has stunning red stalks, worthy of inclusion in the border in their own right. There are also prettily coloured, flowering runner beans, which can add height at the back of the border, and courgettes, with their spectacular exotic-looking, edible yellow flowers, in addition to their stripy fruits.

✤ Although growing vegetables in the border is convenient and attractive, as well as producing useful edible crops, the work and thought involved should not be underestimated. The vegetables will compete with the ornamentals for food, light and water, so never overcrowd when planting. Ideally, consider the ornamentals as the adjuncts to the edibles, not the other way around, so that the vegetables are given the best possible growing conditions.

## COMPANION PLANTING

F ASCINATING work has been done on companion planting, which means growing plants side by side for their positive effects on each other, whether directly or indirectly. It is worth researching this subject further, particularly if you are planning to grow edibles and ornamentals together.

✤ Combining certain flowers and edible crops often has significant benefits, particularly in assisting pest and disease control. For example, garlic is an excellent friend to roses, since it is reputed to deter aphids as well as

improving the roses' perfume. Equally importantly, research on companion planting reveals that some combinations have a detrimental effect on each other, for example garlic planted alongside peas and beans.

ABOVE: *A well-tended vegetable plot can yield a wonderful array of crops that will sustain you throughout the year.*

BELOW: *A neatly planted allotment growing strawberries, chives and shallots to ripen in the early summer.*

ABOVE: *Some fruit trees make attractive and productive container plants.*

need other trees around it for pollination. For example, if you have the space and inclination for only a single apple tree in a container, you will need a dwarf rootstock, such as M27 or M9, with a 'family' of three or four compatible varieties grafted on to it so that no further trees are needed for pollination.

### Suitable containers

❀ Choose your container with due consideration to the needs of the plant you are growing. Fruit trees prefer a free root run, so will need generously proportioned containers. Cherries, plums, pears, apples and the like need containers that are at least 38 cm (15 in) deep, preferably much deeper.

❀ Dustbins, although not the most attractive of containers, make perfect homes for container-grown fruit trees. You could choose a galvanised metal one for industrial chic, or wrap bamboo or other natural screening around an inexpensive plastic bin. The latter option has the added advantage that you could easily conceal a layer of plastic bubble wrap beneath the decorative natural wrapping for added winter insulation.

❀ There are also very attractive large containers that once served quite different purposes, for example old washing tubs, which look like giant Chinese lanterns made of silvery metal that has softened in tone over the years.

## GROWING FRUIT IN CONTAINERS

GROWING fruit in containers has grown in popularity in recent years. Even gardeners with diminutive plots can produce fruit crops that taste wonderful, are free of chemicals, rich in nutrients and absolutely fresh. Most fruiting plants are also extremely decorative as well as productive. For example, apple trees are often grown as much for their ornamental virtues as for their edible fruits. Strawberries possess a convenient tumbling growth habit, ideally suited to hanging baskets as well as the multi-holed terracotta pots that are more familiar as strawberry planters.

❀ Choose your species carefully when planting fruit in containers, especially if growing fruit trees. The plant should be clearly labelled in the garden centre or nursery, with full details of its rootstock, how much space it requires, and whether it is self-fertilising or will

RIGHT: *Strawberries reward even minimal care with generous crops of juicy, ripe fruit.*

## Caring for container-grown fruit

❁ The container fruit gardener needs to pay special attention to planting, watering, feeding and potting on, particularly if growing trees in containers. One useful way of reducing the effort involved in potting on every two years or so is to plant in a container that is initially oversized, lifting up the plant when necessary and adding further layers of compost beneath the first until the plant eventually outgrows the container. Plant with a good organic potting compost.

❁ Ideally, arrange some sort of permanent watering system for containers, to save work and ensure that the compost doesn't dry out. To give an idea of the watering needs of a container-grown fruit tree, you may find that in hot weather it needs a drink three or four times a day! Clearly, it is worth investing in a system that makes this an achievable proposition. Watering is not generally needed during winter.

## Fruits for container growing

❁ For the best chance of success, always choose fruits with a good track record as container-grown plants. Strawberries are a perennial favourite and can be grown in all sorts of containers. Even individual small pots of strawberries on a windowsill will produce a good yield. Growing strawberries in containers has the additional benefit of reducing the risk of slug attack and removing

ABOVE: *Figs thrive in containers, since they like having their roots restricted.*

the need for the laborious mulching and weeding that is required when growing strawberries in the ground.

❁ Figs make good container plants, since they like having their roots restricted. Conversely, grapes hate root restriction and never do well in containers. Apples are a better choice than pears, since pears are not available on dwarf rootstocks at the time of writing, and even the smallest grows to at least 2.4 m (8 ft) tall.

❁ Some fruits are perfectly happy in containers, but their growth habit makes them too untidy a choice for decorative planting, for example raspberries, which grow tall and need staking and netting. Chosen well, watered well and placed in a spot sympathetic to their needs, container-grown fruits will be an attractive and rewarding addition to your garden.

LEFT: *Pear trees do not thrive in containers because they are not available in dwarf rootstocks.*

ABOVE: *A mature holy basil (labiatae) has grown bushy and in a wooden half barrel.*

## GROWING HERBS

HERBS are enjoying a major resurgence in popularity – both as attractive plants and for everyday use in cooking. Of course, herbs have also been used for centuries to decorate and perfume the home, as well as for their medicinal attributes.

❀ Since harvesting herbs regularly actually helps the plants, by keeping them compact and bushy, and encouraging new, fresh, tasty young growth, herb gardens are best placed within reasonable range of the kitchen. You will feel less like tramping down the garden path in the pouring rain for a handful of fresh herbs, than simply reaching out to a window box or herb garden close to the kitchen door.

❀ Herbs make great container plants, since many of them enjoy the well-drained conditions that containers can provide. At one end of the spectrum, a perfectly useful and decorative herb garden can be planted into small pots which, when placed on a sunny windowsill, will provide you with a an easily accessible supply of herbs all year round.

❀ By contrast, twinned tubs flanking your front door and containing elegant standard bay trees with plaited stems are major herb investments that may need winter protection – and even protection against theft. Whatever size of garden you have, you will always be able to find room for a few herbs.

❀ Concentrate on growing a few varieties well, rather than a diversity of species that can quickly grow untidy. Where possible, separate each herb – perhaps by growing each one in an individual container or, as in a traditional herb garden, in distinct compartments.

❀ Many herbs can be quite invasive and vigorous growing. Separating them helps to prevent one herb overwhelming another, looks neat, and enables you to harvest and cultivate one herb without disturbing its neighbour. Divided containers are available specifically for this purpose, or you may have space to plant a knot garden, or herb garden in a wheel formation, with each spoke delineated by bricks or path edging, to create separate sections.

## DIVIDING HERBS AND OTHER SMALL PLANTS

DIVIDING small plants is an excellent way of adding to your stocks at zero expense and with minimal effort. In addition, many perennial plants benefit from being lifted and divided every few years. Left undivided, their middles may start to die out, and the remaining growth can become straggly.

Ease the plant into sections, teasing out the roots gently, rather than tearing them apart. Replant each section and water well. When dividing old plants, discard the weak, old, central section and replant only the fresh young growth around the edges of the plant.

## RESTRICTING THE SPREAD OF MINT

*Invasive and fast growing, mint is best grown in a container in the ground, which will restrict its root spread yet provide adequate moisture. Use a standard pot or bottomless bucket; some gardeners use slate embedded in the ground to restrict the root run.*

**1** Dig a hole large enough for the rim of a generously sized pot to be buried just below ground level.

**2** Place the pot in the ground and bed it firmly into the soil with your hands. Make sure the rim is level with the soil surface.

**3** Add a small amount of potting compost to the bottom of the pot.

**4** Place the mint in the pot and then backfill the pot with compost and firm it around the plant. Water well. Lift, divide and repot the plant each spring.

## STARTING OUT

MANY herb gardens begin with an impulse buy of a healthy, container-grown perennial herb from the wide range of herbs on display at the garden centre, and this can be an excellent start. Although many herbs can be grown from seed, if you need only one example of a herb, such as rosemary, it is cheaper, as well as easier, to buy a single plant. Herbs such as chives, which you may want in larger quantities, for example, to use as a decorative edging or as a companion plant elsewhere in the garden, are easily propagated by division; so just a few plants from the garden centre will quickly yield many more. Some annual herbs, such as nasturtiums and basil, are quick and easy to grow from seed.

## Cultivation requirements

❀ Many herbs are sun lovers, needing at least six hours of sunlight a day in order to thrive. Without good light, they can become thin and straggly, with a poor aroma. Most herbs also dislike being waterlogged, so plant them in well-drained soil. Some, such as thyme, sage and dwarf lavender, are very drought tolerant and actively enjoy sunny, dry conditions. Most herbs prefer warm conditions. Although they can tolerate temperatures of 7°C (45°F), herbs do not thrive in the cold.

❀ Protect cherished perennial herbs such as bay and rosemary against extremely cold or windy weather conditions. A simple way to care for tender herbs is to plant them in containers, plunged into the ground during the milder months and removed for overwintering in a protected environment. Some herbs, such as mint, are very invasive, and are always best planted in containers within the soil so that they do not colonise the garden.

## HARVESTING HERBS

PICK leaves at any time during the growing season. Evergreens such as thyme may be harvested at any time, but allow new growth to harden off before winter.

## PLANTING A CONTAINER HERB GARDEN

**1** *Strawberry pots allow many different herbs to be grown in a small space. Place a layer of crocks at the bottom of the pot. Fill up to the first planting hole with compost mixed with water-retaining gel.*

**2** *Taking care not to disturb the root ball, push the roots of the first herb through the lowest planting hole into the pot.*

**3** *Work up the pot, adding more compost and plants until you reach the top. Plant more herbs in the top of the pot. Water slowly and carefully so that the water reaches into every planting pocket.*

**4** *Each spring, lift and divide any herbs that are growing too large or straggly for the pot.*

- Harvest leaves in the morning, after the dew has evaporated from the foliage. Leaves are at their most flavoursome and tender just before the herb comes into flower. If harvesting the flowers, you should collect these at midday in dry weather, just as the flower is beginning to open fully.
- Take care to keep your harvested herbs loose, and with plenty of air circulating freely around them to prevent bruising, crushing or other deterioration prior to use. Traditional trugs are perfect for collecting herbs.
- Herb seed may be collected when it is fully hardened and ripe, on a warm, dry day. Roots are generally harvested in autumn when the parts of the plant above the ground are starting to die back.
- The active components sought by herbalists for medicinal uses will have developed in the root systems of perennials in the second or third year after planting. Annual roots may be harvested at the end of each year. If you are not planning on using the herbs immediately after picking, then prepare them for preservation as soon as possible after harvesting, for optimum results.

## STORING HERBS

How you handle herbs after harvesting will depend on the type of herb, and its intended use. Some herbs lose a lot of their flavour if dried. The taste and aroma of such herbs is better retained by freezing or by preserving in oil or vinegar.

### Freezing herbs

- Freezing is a simple and effective way of preserving much of the flavour, colour and nutritional content of herbs. Some of the more delicate herbs produce fresher tasting results when frozen rather than dried. Freeze them in labelled plastic bags or rigid containers. Alternatively, freeze small quantities of finely chopped herbs in individual ice cube trays and top up with water for convenient cooking quantities.

### Herb oils and vinegars

- Herbs may be infused in oil or vinegar. These are simple to make; they liven up salads and marinades and make lovely gifts, too. Herb vinegars are also popular in cooking and as hair or skin rinses.

## DRYING YOUR HERBS

*Herbs need to be dried as quickly as possible after harvesting, in order to retain maximum colour and scent. It is important that any moisture is removed before the plant material begins to deteriorate – rotting or becoming mouldy.*

**1** *Pick several stems or leaves of your herb, in this case rosemary. Remove any leaves that would crowd together and hold too much moisture so that they would rot rather than dry out. Make small bunches for quick drying. Hang them upside down in a dry, warm, dark or shaded place is needed, such as an airing cupboard. Allow plenty of air to circulate around the drying herbs.*

**2** *When drying is complete, after one to four weeks, the herbs may be rubbed through a sieve to remove the stalks, or shredded by hand, and bottled. Keep the bottled herbs in a dark, dry place until needed.*

# GROWING AND USING HERBS

*This chart identifies some of the most regularly used herbs. In addition it shows their various uses in cooking and, in some cases, medical treatments and explains how to grow them most effectively.*

## Herb

## Use

## Cultivation

**Basil**

*Used in many popular Italian dishes; natural partner to tomatoes. Roughly tear the leaves, rather than chop*

*Tender annual; cannot withstand frost*

**Bay**

*Prime ingredient of bouquet garni; goes well with fish, stews and rice dishes. Tear the edges of the leaf before adding to a dish, and remove before serving the meal*

*Evergreen shrub; can withstand cold, but benefits from frost and wind protection*

**Borage**

*Delicately flavoured and pretty addition to long summer drinks*

*Hardy annual; grow in a sunny position, in any soil type*

**Chives**

*Mild onion flavour; partners cheese, potatoes, eggs and butter particularly well. Not as rich in sulphur as onions, thus do not have the same tendency to cause digestive disturbance*

*Hardy perennial. Chives left to flower are pretty perennial plants, easily propagated by division. For the tastiest flavour, do not allow the plant to flower*

**Coriander**

*Young leaves are deliciously perfumed and widely used in curries, as are the aromatic seeds*

*Hardy annual; prefers a sunny, well-drained position*

**Dill**

*Partners salmon and other types of fish especially well*

*Hardy annual; grow in a sheltered, cool position in rich, deep soil*

**Feverfew**

*Mainly ornamental; medicinal use as a cure for headache – note, herbal remedies should only ever be taken on the advice of an experienced practitioner*

*Hardy perennial; self-seeds readily. Prefers dry, well-drained soil in a sunny position*

| Herb | Use | Cultivation |
|------|-----|-------------|
| Lavender | Popular culinary ingredient; adds delicate perfumed flavour to honey, and to savoury dishes. Popular in pot pourri, sleep pillows and as decorative flower – fresh and dried | Hardy evergreen; grow in a dry, sunny position; clip after flowering |
| Marjoram | Partners eggs, cheese and tomatoes particularly well | Hardy perennial; grow in moist, sunny position |
| Mint | Used in mint sauce as essential accompaniment to roast lamb | Hardy perennial; grow in moist soil in partial shade or sun. Very invasive, therefore best grown in a container |
| Oregano | Widely used in bouquet garni, stuffings and for sprinkling over meat before roasting | Hardy perennial; grow in a well-drained, sunny position |
| Parsley | Popular garnish; goes particularly well with fish and potatoes | Hardy biennial; grow in slightly sheltered, rich moist soil |
| Rosemary | Traditional accompaniment to lamb and pork | Evergreen; grow in a sunny position in sandy, well-drained soil, preferably in sheltered position |
| Sage | Natural partner to onions; popular as a stuffing to counteract the richness of roast meats | Evergreen; grow in sunny site on light, well-drained soil |
| Thyme | Used in widely in soups and stews, omelettes and salads | Evergreen; grow in light, stony soil in full sun |

# GARDEN PROJECTS

**If you love the idea of container gardening, but need a little inspiration to get you going, you'll find plenty on the following pages.**

Start with an unusual idea, a citronella candle pot – not strictly speaking a 'gardening' project, but one that will definitely add to the enjoyment of your garden as evening falls, with its quota of mosquitoes!

There are fabulous ideas for making your own containers for different purposes, and if you're short of cash, fake it – transform a cheap plastic chimney pot with a stunning faux lead finish.

# CANDLE POTS

These terracotta flowerpots gain a shot of glamour with a shimmering of gold around their rims. Not only does the candlelight add sparkle to outdoor entertaining, but a generous dash of citronella essential oil in the candle wax deters annoying insect invasion as dusk falls.

## TOOLS AND MATERIALS

- Small paintbrushes
- Acrylic gold size
- Terracotta flowerpot
- Scissors
- Gold-coloured Dutch metal leaf
- Soft bristled brush
- Amber shellac
- Modelling clay
- Wick
- Pencil or thin twig
- Candle wax
- Bain-marie (double boiler)
- Candle colourant (optional)
- Citronella essential oil

**1** Brush acrylic gold size around the rims of the flowerpot and leave to dry until transparent, but not so dry that it has lost its adhesive property. The length of time this takes will depend on the ambient temperature and humidity and may be anything between 10 and 30 minutes – some acrylic size has an indefinite 'open' or working time, making it foolproof to use.

**2** Cut the metal leaf into manageable pieces. Place the metal leaf on the sized area and gently ease into place using a soft bristled brush. Gently brush away excess leaf. Continue until all of the sized area has been gilded.

**3** Apply a coat of amber shellac to the gilded area to form a protective seal. Leave to dry, following the manufacturer's directions.

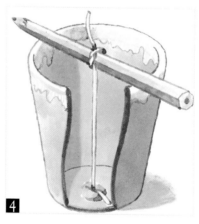

**4** Push a small piece of modelling clay into the drainage hole at the bottom of the flowerpot to seal it. Suspend the candle wick centrally in the pot by attaching the upper end of the wick to a pencil or twig laid across the top of the pot. Embed part of the bottom of the wick in the modelling clay, allowing the remaining part to lie across the bottom of the pot so that the finished candle will burn for as long as possible.

**5** Melt the candle wax in a bain-marie (double boiler). Add candle colourant if desired, and a few drops of citronella essential oil.

**6** Pour the molten wax into the flowerpot and leave until set, then snip the wick with scissors.

# WIRE BASKET WALL PLANTER

It is easy to make a whole collection of wall planters that are cost effective and also easily outclass their plastic-coated, mass-produced counterparts. The gentle tones and textures of wire and hessian are a natural, understated partner to any planting. You should always wear stout protective gloves when working with chicken wire, which has very sharp edges.

## TOOLS AND MATERIALS

- Pencil and paper, for template
- Scissors
- 12 mm (½ in) exterior-grade ply-wood
- Jigsaw
- Stout protective gloves
- Protective eye goggles
- Floristry scissors or wire cutters, for cutting chicken wire
- Chicken wire
- Hessian
- Netting staples
- Staple gun or hammer
- Length of wire

**1** Draw a symmetrical basket shape on a piece of paper, slightly shallower than a semicircle. Cut out the paper template. Place it on your piece of plywood and draw around it. Cut out the wooden shape, using a jigsaw.

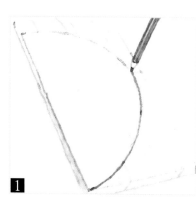

**2** Wearing protective gloves and eye goggles and using floristry scissors

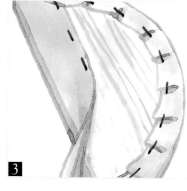

or wire cutters, roughly cut out a piece of chicken wire to fit the plywood, allowing plenty extra to wrap around behind the wooden shape, as well as sufficient to make a pocket at the front. Cut a piece of hessian to the same size as the chicken wire.

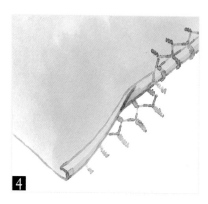

**3** Cut a second piece of hessian large enough to wrap around the plywood. Wrap it around one face of the shaped plywood and staple it in place on the back, tucking the edges of the hessian under neatly as you work. (The stapled side will be inside the back of the basket.)

**4** Take the remaining piece of hessian and fold under one long edge twice to form a neat 'hem'. Fold the raw edge of one long side of the chicken wire around the folded edge of hessian to produce a tidy, firmly rolled 'hem', which will be the top edge of the basket.

**5** Shape the hessian and chicken wire roughly to produce a pocket of the desired size ion the front face of the plywood (i.e. the one that is not completely covered by hessian). The bare plywood will be inside the basket and therefore concealed as the pocket is filled with compost.

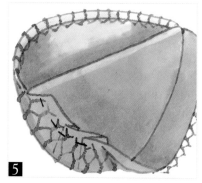

**6** Secure the pocket in place by stapling the edges of the hessian and wire on to the wooden shape. Keep placing your hand inside the pocket as it is formed to ensure that you produce an even, symmetrical shape.

**7** Trim away excess hessian and chicken wire. Staple the ends of a length of wire to the back corners of the basket to make a loop for hanging the planter on the wall.

# CHIMNEY POT PLANTER

This elegant planter started life in a much less sophisticated guise –
as an orange-coloured plastic chain store bargain. A simple paint
technique transforms the fake terracotta into a deceptively realistic faux
lead finish, which complements plants beautifully.

## TOOLS AND MATERIALS

- Medium grade sandpaper
- Plastic chimney pot planter
- Spray can of white acrylic primer
- Matt emulsion paint in white and charcoal grey
- Paintbrush
- Acrylic scumble glaze
- Plastic carton
- Spray can of exterior acrylic varnish, in matt or satin finish

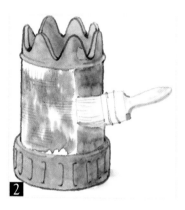

**1** *Using medium grade sandpaper, sand the plastic planter well so as to provide a 'key' for the paint, enabling it to adhere well. Working in a well-ventilated area, spray the planter evenly with white acrylic primer – all over the outside and on the inside at the top of the planter.*

**2** *When the first coat of primer has dried sufficiently (follow the manufacturer's directions for drying and re-application times), apply a second coat of white acrylic primer – sufficient to cover the planter uniformly. Leave to dry thoroughly – preferably overnight.*

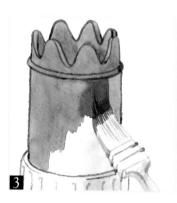

**3** *Paint the planter evenly with charcoal-grey emulsion paint and leave to dry for at least 3 hours.*

**4** *Place a little acrylic scumble glaze in a plastic carton and tint it with white emulsion paint. Add water until the glaze has a runny, milky consistency. Briskly brush the glaze all over the planter, allowing the glaze to run unevenly down the surfaces, forming pools that are opaque in some areas and watery and translucent in others. Wash randomly over the glaze with a little water, taking care not to dislodge the glaze in areas where it has formed naturalistic patterns. Leave to dry for several hours.*

**5** *Add more of the same glaze to some areas of the planter to give an impression of age-encrusted salts. Add water to soften any hard, unnatural lines. Flick splatters of the glaze randomly over some parts of the planter to give a further weathered impression. Leave to dry thoroughly – preferably overnight.*

**6** *Working in a well-ventilated area, finish the planter by spraying it with acrylic varnish. Apply several coats, following the manufacturer's directions for drying and re-application times.*

# PLANTED BUCKET

Metal complements plants beautifully and it weathers attractively, too. For impromptu entertaining, this hanging bucket can be filled with cut flowers arranged in wet oasis to enliven a garden wall, then later planted up for a more permanent display. The project is as ecologically sound as it is pretty, since this bucket has been recycled, now enjoying a new lease of life after its initial incarnation as a candle pot.

## TOOLS AND MATERIALS

- Hammer
- Long nail
- Small galvanised bucket
- Wallplug plus masonry screw, or wood screw, as appropriate
- Screwdriver
- Plants and compost or cut flowers and wet oasis (florist's foam)

**1** *Using a hammer and a long nail, punch a hole in the side of the galvanised bucket near the rim for hanging the planter.*

**2** *In the same way, punch drainage holes through the base of the bucket.*

**3** *Hang the bucket in place, using appropriate fixings – a wallplug and screw for masonry, or just a screw for wood, as here.*

**4** *Plant up the bucket or arrange cut flowers in well-soaked wet oasis for a temporary, colourful display.*

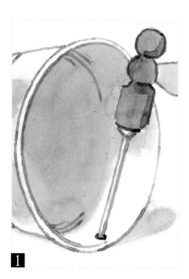

# VERSAILLES-STYLE PLANTER

Supermarkets and do-it-yourself stores are great places to pick up inexpensive growing kits, which come complete with compost, bulbs or seeds and even a planting diagram to ensure a naturalistic display with minimum effort. However, the containers supplied with these kits are all too often unsightly orange 'terracotta-effect' plastic. This smart wooden cover pops neatly over the cheap and cheerful container, has just enough space left around the base for excess water to drain away and is sturdy and attractive enough to use year after year. If using paint rather than woodstain, use an all-in-one formulation, which combines primer, undercoat and topcoat.

## TOOLS AND MATERIALS

- Tape measure
- Plastic planting trough
- Pencil
- Straight edge
- Panel saw
- 12 mm (½ in) exterior-grade plywood
- Exterior wood glue
- 50 x 50 mm (2 x 2 in) planed softwood
- 8 corner joining blocks
- 32 x 12 mm (½ in) No. 6 wood screws
- Screwdriver
- Carpenter's square
- 50 mm (2 in) diameter turned knobs
- Hot melt glue and glue gun (optional)
- Medium/fine sanding block and sandpaper
- Damp rag
- Exterior paint or woodstain
- Paintbrush

**2** Cut four corner posts of 50 x 50 mm (2 x 2 in) planed softwood, 60 mm (2⅜ in) taller than the height of the plastic planter.

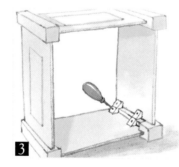

**4** When all four panels and corner posts have been assembled, glue a decorative knob on the top of each corner post, using hot melt glue or exterior wood glue.

**5** Sand all surfaces lightly and smooth off any rough edges with a sanding block. Rub off sanding dust with a damp rag.

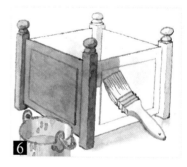

**1** Measure the height and width of the plastic planter to be disguised. Cut four plywood panels 10 mm (⅜ in) wider and 20 mm (¾ in) taller than the plastic planter. Cut four plywood panels smaller than the first panels by 100 mm (4 in) all round and glue these in the middle of the first panels, using exterior wood glue.

**3** With the smaller decorative plywood panels facing outwards, fix the panels to the corner posts, using corner joining blocks and wood screws. Align the bottom edge of the panels 10 mm (⅜ in) up from the bottom of the corner posts, to leave a small gap at the base of the planter so that the water can drain away.

**6** Paint the planter using exterior paint or woodstain. Apply at least two coats, allowing drying times between coats according to the manufacturer's instructions.

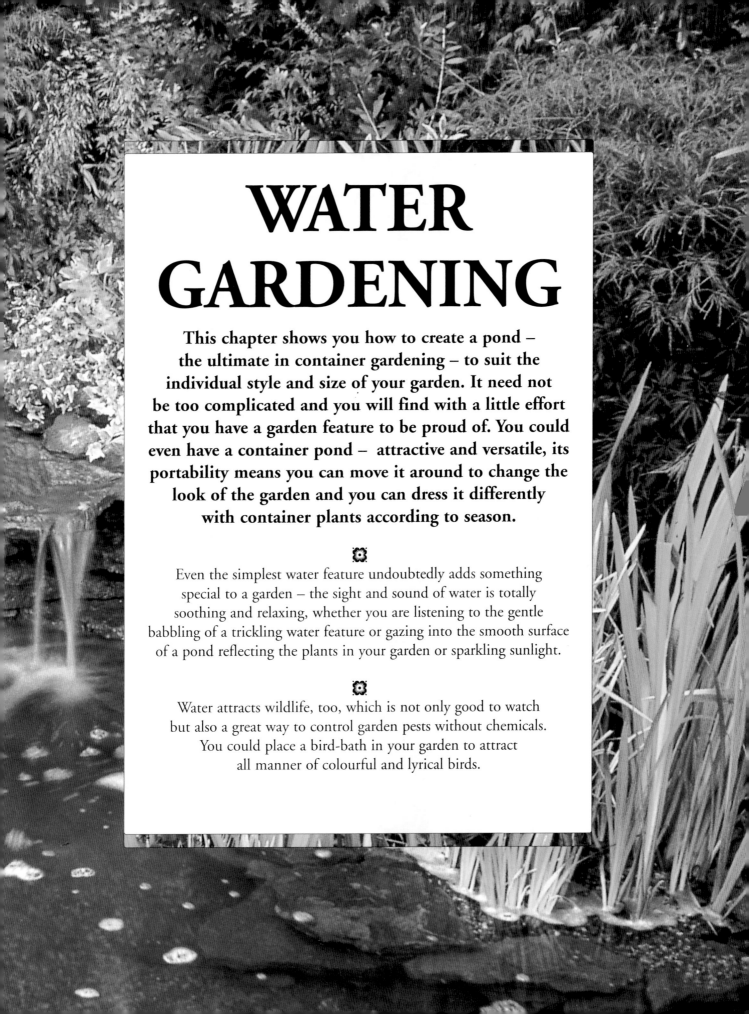

# WATER GARDENING

**This chapter shows you how to create a pond –
the ultimate in container gardening – to suit the
individual style and size of your garden. It need not
be too complicated and you will find with a little effort
that you have a garden feature to be proud of. You could
even have a container pond – attractive and versatile, its
portability means you can move it around to change the
look of the garden and you can dress it differently
with container plants according to season.**

❖

Even the simplest water feature undoubtedly adds something
special to a garden – the sight and sound of water is totally
soothing and relaxing, whether you are listening to the gentle
babbling of a trickling water feature or gazing into the smooth surface
of a pond reflecting the plants in your garden or sparkling sunlight.

❖

Water attracts wildlife, too, which is not only good to watch
but also a great way to control garden pests without chemicals.
You could place a bird-bath in your garden to attract
all manner of colourful and lyrical birds.

# BUILDING PONDS

Water, contained or moving, is a fabulous addition to any garden.
Even the smallest plot can accommodate a water feature, even if it is as
simple as a wall-mounted spout trickling water into a small ornamental
trough. The sound of moving water is incredibly tranquil, and gazing into
the reflections of a pond is also very calming. Do not be put off
by the technical aspects of water gardening. There are ways of
incorporating water into a garden design that need no complex
wiring or plumbing arrangements. For example, simply adding
a bird-bath and keeping it topped up with a watering can
is a feature that will attract birds to your garden.

### Water and wildlife

❀ Many gardeners introduce water features because they
want to encourage wildlife to come into the garden.
This has many significant benefits beyond the
immediate pleasures of watching frogs leaping around
the pond, or birds enjoying a morning bath.

BELOW: *A fountain adds interest to a geometric pond.*

❀ Introducing wildlife to your garden moves you closer to
an organic gardening style – that is, gardening using all
the forces of nature to optimum effect. Birds, animals
and insects will be attracted by a ready supply of water,
and will repay you by assisting in pest control and by
improving soil fertility.
❀ Birds will not only amuse you with their antics in your
bird-bath, but also devour pests such as wireworms and
leatherjackets and improve soil fertility by adding their
droppings, and eventually their bodies when they die,
to produce humus. Birds with good access to water will
also eat less of your berries and fruits.

## CONTAINER PONDS

CONTAINER ponds are a brilliant introduction to water
gardening, and are wonderfully adaptable to
individual needs. Even if you are gardening outside a fifth-
floor apartment, on an area little bigger than a fire escape,
you can still have a pond. Another great attribute of self-
contained ponds is that they are portable. You can move
one around to change the look of the garden, in the same
way that you dress it differently throughout the seasons
with container plants. You can also take it with you when
you move house.

### Choosing containers

❀ A wide variety of containers are suitable, such as glazed
pots in aquatic tones of cobalt blue or viridian, or half-
barrels, which look very comfortable in cottage-style
settings. Plants can include miniature water lilies,
which prefer still water, combined with marginal and

ABOVE: *There is a pond style to suit every gardening taste – this Oriental-looking pond is full of koi carp.*

oxygenating plants, while goldfish can dart prettily in and out of the foliage. If you are using a metal container, make sure that it is not of a type that will leach rust into the water, as this can harm plants and fish. Painting a galvanised container with black bituminous paint will render it safe.

✿ It may sound obvious, but always choose a container that is leakproof. Ask to have the container filled with water if you are in any doubt as to its watertightness. Risking momentary embarrassment will save a lot of aggravation later. Small containers look unattractive if you need to line them with something. Although you can drain a leaking container and seal it internally with a proprietary sealant before painting it with bituminous paint, this is not a job most gardeners would actively seek to undertake.

## Winter care

✿ Ideally, bring a ceramic container pond under cover for winter, as it may crack if the water in it freezes and then expands. Alternatively, drain and store it upside down if keeping it outside, so that it does not fill with rainwater, which may also freeze and cause cracking.

✿ Barrel ponds are made of wood, which is a natural insulator, so can be left out of doors in sheltered conditions. However, pay attention to the individual needs of the fish and plants in all types of container pond. Even if the wood does not crack in freezing conditions, the fish may not be so resilient.

BELOW: *Here water is piped in steps from a spouting fountain in one ceramic container to a second and on into a third.*

## PERMANENT PONDS

SINCE permanent ponds are designed to be just that, it is well worth taking a really careful look at all the factors that need to be considered before starting work. It can be all too easy to be swayed into buying a liner that has been made into an attractively landscaped pond in a garden centre, but which may be quite unsuitable in the site available in your own garden, so do plan thoroughly before purchasing.

### Size

❀ To keep the water clear, and to sustain a reasonable amount of wildlife such as several different types of fish, you will need a pond with a minimum depth of 60 cm (24 in), with a water surface of at least 3.7 sq m (40 sq ft).

### Site

❀ Ideally, site a pond in an area that receives at least six hours of sunlight each day, is sheltered from easterly winds, and not close to deciduous trees, which will shower it with leaves every autumn. Decayed leaves produce gases and salts that are hazardous to fish, and encourage green algae.

❀ Ponds can obviously be positioned in shady sites, and the reflections on the surface of the water can light up a dull corner, but most pond plants need good light in order to thrive. A water feature without organic elements, for example a fountain or waterspout, is a better choice in a shady spot.

BELOW: *Ponds thrive best in areas that receive six hours sunlight a day. You can brighten the area further with plants in colourful containers.*

❀ If you are planning to incorporate moving water within your pond, you will need access to electricity. Although you can have an electricity supply installed where it is needed, you may find the cost precludes this option.

❀ Rather than surrender your dream of a cascading fountain entirely, you may reach a compromise by siting your pond close to a mains power source, such as an outbuilding or the house itself. Solar-powered pumps are another option. At the time of writing, they are in their infancy, expensive and with power that diminishes as light levels drop. However, they are an ecologically

BELOW: *Ponds can be as big or small as the space in a garden dictates.*

sound development, and of particular interest to gardeners without access to external power supplies.

## Shape and style

❀ Choose a shape that harmonises with the rest of your garden. A pond that mimics a natural pool, complete with rocky outcrops and alpine planting, is all too often the automatic choice of the novice water gardener; yet it may look hopelessly incongruous in an austere, modern setting. Conversely, a small, higgledy-piggledy cottage-style garden would look very uncomfortable with a ferociously geometric formal pool at its centre.

## Safety

❀ Any amount of standing water poses a potential drowning hazard, especially to a small child. The only truly child-friendly water features are those with no standing water, such as pebble fountains.

❀ However, it is possible to render a conventional pond childproof by covering the water with a strong metal grid, which may be concealed by growing plants through it. The grid can be removed when your children have grown up, but remember that your uncovered pond is also dangerous to any visiting children, who will be particularly attracted by the novelty of unfamiliarity.

## MAKING A LINED POND

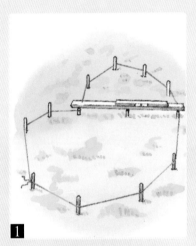

**1**

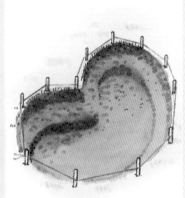

**3**

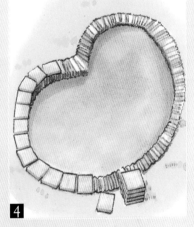

**2**

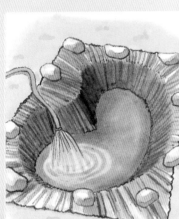

**4**

**2** Excavate the hole, initially working around the edge to a depth of approximately 30 cm (12 in) to produce a planting shelf for marginal plants. Continue by digging out the central part of the pond, leaving the planting shelf the same width as its depth. Remove any roots, rocks and debris from the base of the pond, since these may puncture the liner.

**3** Place the liner across the hole and leave it to settle for an hour or so. Making sure that the liner is centred over the hole, place stones around its edges to weigh it down. Fill the pond with slow-running water, allowing the liner to settle evenly into the hole. Gradually remove the stones from the edge of the liner as the pond fills. Fold the liner neatly, if necessary, to incorporate any corners.

**4** Remove the stones and trim the liner with scissors, leaving a 15-cm (6-in) 'fringe' all the way around. Lay edging stones on a mortar base around the perimeter of the pond to conceal the excess liner.

**1** Mark out the required pond shape on the ground, using a hose or string and pegs.

Measure the area of the pond to calculate the amount of flexible pond liner required (see over).

## CHOOSING POND LINERS

TRADITIONALLY, puddled clay was used to retain water in ponds, but it is not a reliable or convenient lining method. Concrete is still used in some commercial applications, but is costly and laborious to install. Most modern water gardeners choose between rigid and flexible liners when installing a pond.

❀ Preformed liners can be expensive, and their 'ready-made' look is deceptive. They are actually more difficult to install than flexible liners, which are brilliantly versatile.

❀ Always buy the best-quality liner you can afford, so that you don't need to replace it in a hurry. This is particularly important if you are planning a large, complex water garden, full of fish and plants, which would be time-consuming and tedious to dismantle for liner repair or replacement.

## RIGID LINERS

PREFORMED liners are an extremely popular choice, but the cheaper, more commonly used semi-rigid preformed liners actually move about as you are trying to fit them, making installation very difficult. Any inaccuracy in fitting is soon cruelly revealed as water gathers at one end or, worse still, the liner cracks as it is forced to try and hold a great weight of water at a point that is not sufficiently supported beneath the liner. They are also short-lived, lasting only five to 10 years. They are generally too shallow for overwintering fish, unless you use a pond heater. They are also too shallow for many plants. Truly rigid liners are much more expensive, and do last for 25 years or more if installed properly; but for most situations, a good-quality flexible liner is a better choice.

ABOVE: *A well-maintained pond brings a whole new dimension to gardening.*

## FLEXIBLE LINERS

WITH a flexible liner you can create a truly customised pond, shaped as you wish, with appropriate depth for all the plants and fish that you want. Mark out the shape on the ground using a line of sand, a hose or rope to get a feel for your design before you commit to it. To calculate the amount of flexible liner needed, measure the length and width of the desired pond. Add double the maximum depth of the pond to each measurement. For an irregularly shaped pond, follow the same process, first fitting the irregular shape into an imaginary rectangle to determine its rough size.

### Butyl rubber

❀ This is wonderfully forgiving and tolerant, easy to install, flexible, and will even adapt over time as the soil beneath it settles. As long as it is not punctured by careless handling or animal attack, it will last for at least 25 years, a major plus if you are installing a complicated water feature.

### Long-life PVC

❀ Not as expensive as butyl rubber, this material has been chemically treated to enhance its flexibility so that it will resist cracking in sunlight. Some liners classified as long-life PVC have been nylon reinforced, which does strengthen them, but does not necessarily make them less brittle. Both types should last up to 25 years.

### PVC

❀ PVC is really suitable only for lining a bog garden, where the liner will be totally concealed from the sun, since PVC becomes brittle after repeated sun exposure, and will start to crack around the edges where it is not covered with water.

❀ Although punctures in flexible liners beneath the water can be repaired, it is not possible to repair cracks around the pond's rim satisfactorily. PVC is inexpensive and may be an option if you are installing a water feature destined to be very short-lived. The average life expectancy of a PVC liner is between five and 10 years.

### Black polythene

❀ Do not be tempted to use cheap black polythene as a pond liner, not even for a bog garden. It is simply not substantial enough, and will last for only two or three years at the most.

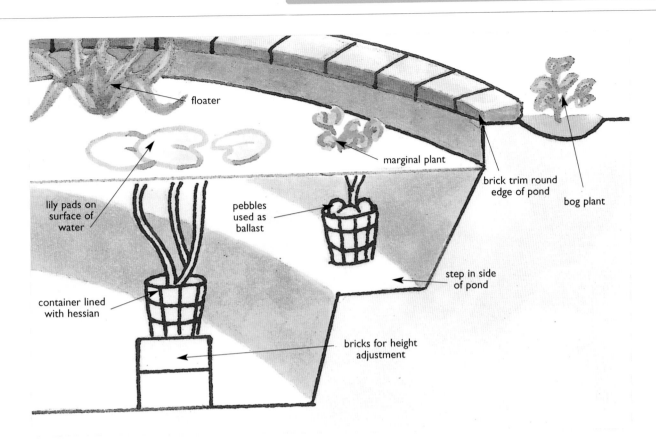

floater

marginal plant

lily pads on surface of water

pebbles used as ballast

brick trim round edge of pond

bog plant

step in side of pond

container lined with hessian

bricks for height adjustment

ABOVE: *Cross-section of a stepped and lined permanent pond, showing planting features.*

## PLANTING UP A POND BASKET

**1** Use a container of adequate size for the root system of the fully grown plant. Unless it is of very fine mesh, line the container with hessian. Add moist aquatic soil to the container and place the plant on top. Backfill with more aquatic soil, firming it in.

**2** To weight down the container and prevent soil dispersing into the water, add a top dressing of gravel.

**3** Cut away any excess hessian and fix string handles to the rim of the container to help you lower it into position in the pond. If the plant is too immature and light to stay anchored below the surface of the water, add more gravel or large pebbles as ballast until the plant grows bigger.

**1**

**2**

**3**

# MAINTAINING A POND

*Your pond will require various maintenance tasks, depending on the season.*

## Spring

❀ Feed fish according to their individual needs when you notice that they have become active.

❀ Check that all electrical components of your water feature are in good working order.

❀ Remove, clean and store your pond heater.

❀ Reconnect the submersible pump on your fountain or waterfall.

❀ Lift, divide and replant new portions of congested water lilies and other overcrowded plants.

❀ Start to plant new aquatics.

❀ Fertilise established aquatic plants, following the manufacturer's directions explicitly so that you do not inadvertently feed the algae rather than the cultivated plants.

## Autumn

❀ As long as fish appear active, continue feeding.

❀ Continue planting until the weather begins to grow cooler.

❀ Continue lifting, dividing and replanting new portions of overcrowded plants until the colder weather arrives.

❀ Cut down and remove the foliage and flower stems of plants as they fade, having first checked the individual needs of each plant. For example, marginal plants should not be cut down below the water level.

❀ Remove debris from the pond regularly.

❀ Screen the pond by placing mesh netting over the surface, if necessary, to keep out leaves until neighbouring trees are bare.

❀ Remove tender plants and overwinter them in water in a cool, but frost-free environment.

❀ Remove, clean and store the submersible pump.

❀ Install the pond heater.

## Summer

❀ Continue feeding the fish, following the food manufacturer's directions precisely.

❀ Continue planting.

❀ Monitor the water level and top up as necessary. In hot conditions, the level can drop 2.5–5 cm (1–2 in) in a week, which can make a real difference in a small pond, and is obviously hazardous to plants, fish and the pond liner. If you are going away for a long period, have a friend keep an eye on the water level in your absence and top it up if necessary.

❀ Remove blanket weed from the surface of the water using a rake or by winding it on to a stick.

❀ Deadhead faded flower heads before they set seed.

## Winter

❀ Stop feeding the fish.

❀ Stop planting.

❀ Take precautionary measures against the worst of the winter weather. Float a ball on the surface of the water if you do not have a pond heater to prevent ice forming. In a small pool, the whole pond can become frozen, which is lethal for fish and many plants. In larger ponds, the ice itself is not a killer, but if the surface of the water is covered with ice for more than a day or so, the toxic methane gas released from submerged, decaying vegetation is allowed to build up and can be lethal to fish. Keeping a small area of the pond free of ice permits the gas to disperse into the air.

## Treating leaks

❀ If a pond is losing more water than you would expect from normal levels of evaporation, you will need to investigate further. Temporarily house fish and plants elsewhere during your explorations.

❀ If you have a fountain or other water course fitted, turn off the pump and see if the water level drops, since most leaks occur around the cascade part. If no leak is visible here, or if you do not have a water course fitted, top up the pond and allow the water level to drop naturally until you see the leak. The planting shelf is another common site of leaks.

❀ Sudden, dramatic water loss indicates a major hole, which will need to be fixed in a similar way to repairing a puncture on a bicycle tyre. Use a kit appropriate to the type of liner you have.

❀ If all efforts to find the leak prove fruitless, you may need to put a replacement liner over the old one.

## Leaks in newly installed ponds

❀ Check that the edges of the pond are level. The problem may simply be caused by gravity – the water flowing out of the pond at its lowest point. Another potential problem, which is easily rectified, is that a fold in a flexible liner may be forming a lip, over which water is running, away from the pond. A quick adjustment will stop the leak instantly.

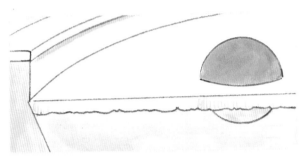

ABOVE: *Float a ball in a newly made pond to ensure that the edges are level – if they are not the ball will naturally drift to the lower edge.*

## MENDING A MAJOR HOLE IN A POND

*If water is lost suddenly from a pond, this indicates a major hole has formed in the liner.*

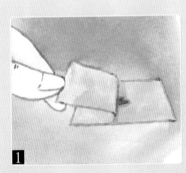

**1** *Locate the hole and find a repair kit to suit the lining of the pond. Place glue over and around the hole in the pond liner. Smear the glue on the patch. Allow to firm up.*

**2** *Place the patch firmly on the glue over the hole in the liner, press down and seal. Allow to harden.*

## MAINTENANCE

*Planted ponds need maintenance to remain healthy and attractive.*

**1** *Cut away yellowing leaves with a sharp knife.*

**2** *Remove blanketweed by revolving a stick in the water.*

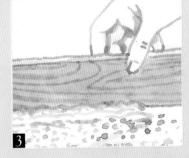

**3** *Skim off duckweed by drawing a plank across the water's surface.*

## INSTALLATION

WATER and electricity are always a combination to be taken seriously where safety is concerned. Low-voltage pumps are available, but are suitable only for small-scale features as they have limited power. Solar-powered pumps are also an option, but are not yet realistic alternatives to mains-powered systems because of their high initial cost and intermittent power in changing weather conditions.

❀ If you are in any doubt at all about installing an electrically powered water feature, use a qualified electrician familiar with this type of work.

❀ A mains cable needs to be run through a conduit pipe to protect it from damage. The conduit is concealed beneath the soil, decking or paving. Always fit a residual current device (RCD), which will cause the power to cut out immediately should there be an interruption to the supply.

❀ Alternatively, have armoured cable and a weatherproof outdoor box with permanently wired-in cables professionally installed.

BELOW: *Water features can incorporate seemingly humble household materials with style and wit.*

## TYPES OF MOVING WATER FEATURE

MOVING water can be incorporated within a pond or pool, or can be a self-contained fountain. Fountains are a particularly useful way of introducing water in difficult situations. Confined spaces that cannot house ponds can almost always offer a vertical surface for a self-contained wall-mounted fountain. In addition, many types of fountains and streams run off over pebbles or slates, so that there is no standing water, which might pose a drowning hazard for small children.

### Fountains

❀ There are many different types of jet available, which fit on the outlet on the top of a submersible pump, to produce a variety of effects. Even a pump with no jet fitted will produce an attractive ripple of water. Choose a jet pattern that is suited your chosen water feature and its surroundings.

## CHOOSING A PUMP

SUBMERSIBLE pumps are suitable for most applications. They are installed at the lowest part of the system, but not on the bottom of the pond where they would draw in the sediment that collects there and quickly become blocked. An upturned pond basket makes a good support.

Buy the best-quality pump you can afford. The pump included as part of an inexpensive fountain kit may be of such low power that the water cascade turns out to be no more than a dispiriting dribble. If the fountain or water feature itself appeals, and it is reasonably priced, consider buying a better pump to replace the one sold with the kit.

If you're creating your own moving water feature, it is worth buying your pump from a reputable specialist water garden supplier, who is dealing with pumps all the time and will be able to advise you as to the most appropriate pump for your needs. Pumps have differing outputs, and these should be clearly marked on the packaging. The output determines how high the pump can propel the water. Clearly, a small bubble fountain does not need a powerful pump, but if you are planning a large fountain that incorporates a gusher jet, you will need more power.

ABOVE: *An ingenious cobble fountain, using large slabs of stone to give a generous flow of water over the cobbles and a lovely splashing sound.*

✿ For example, a bell-jet fountain may look very appealing in the quiet shelter of an enclosed garden centre display, but the neat, bell-shaped fall of water will not be consistent in an exposed, windy position. A foam jet would be a better choice in this situation. All jets are prone to blockage to some degree, so site your fountain where you can easily access the jets for routine maintenance.

## Waterfalls

✿ Waterfalls are not as popular as fountains, largely because they are not generally self-contained and they are more difficult to incorporate within a garden scheme in a convincing way. Ideally, a waterfall should appear totally natural and in harmony with its environment. A good way of introducing a waterfall is to have it linking two streams together. Be especially careful about landscaping a waterfall. Think about how it will look when the water is turned off. It is all too easy to create a concrete edifice that looks like a miniature quarry rather than an idyllic alpine vista.

## CHOOSING THE TYPE OF JET

ALTHOUGH narrow jets of water can sometimes be effective spouting from an informal pool, fountains tend to be more suited to formal layouts. Stone fountains suit symmetrical balance, paved paths, clipped hedges and straight edges. Small, enclosed medieval gardens often had paved paths leading to a fountain in the centre.

However, a fountain jet in an informal pond or a terrace pool will help to oxygenate the water. A few hours of fountain operation in a small pool on a hot summer's day will greatly enhance the oxygen level for fish and plants.

You can diminish turbulence on the water surface by using certain types of jet. For example, a bell jet confines the spray to a very small area of a pool's surface, and will not disturb the leaves of water lilies.

# UNUSUAL PLANTS

**Terracotta pots, old wheelbarrows, hanging
baskets, barrels and other containers often display
a similar range of plants – polyanthus, pelargoniums,
ivies and herbs all make regular appearances.**

But why not plant something a little more original?
Make a pond the focus of your garden and plant water lilies
and flowering marginal plants, with their fantastic shapes
and colours, for an unusual look. Even the pond itself can be
created from a container – try an old trough with dwarf water lilies.

Or it may simply be that your growing conditions are not ideal
for conventional container plants – in a very shady garden,
for example, you might consider growing a wonderful
collection of ferns instead. The colours are fresh
and the shapes are extraordinary.

For a real display of exuberance, choose exotic plants,
such as cacti and succulents, or a grouping of ornamental
grasses or bamboos – this chapter will inspire you to be different!

# GROWING FERNS AND MOISTURE-LOVING PLANTS

❧

**Ferns are among the most delicate-looking of foliage plants. They grow in many different shapes and sizes and can add texture and atmosphere to many parts of the garden. They can enliven and cheer places the sun seldom reaches, act as foils to flowering plants and look very much at home grown in drifts as ground cover in woodland areas. They are particularly at home by streams and in damp, shady corners, and are therefore good for small courtyards. All in all, ferns offer an enormous variety of plants of invaluable use in a modern garden.**

## CHARACTERISTICS

FERNS may be evergreen or deciduous and they have leaf-like fronds, which usually begin to appear in spring. The young fronds, known as crosiers, are tightly curled and unfurl with great grace and beauty as they grow.

❀ The fronds of most ferns grow from rhizomes. These are coated in a furry, scaly covering, which may be black, brown or silvery white. Most rhizomes extend above and below ground, sometimes for a long distance. *Matteuccia struthiopteris* produces crowns of fronds at intervals along its rhizomes.

❀ Rather than producing flowers or seeds, ferns release tiny spores from capsules on the undersides of their fronds. You can often see these as brown markings on the backs of the fronds. These will germinate if given the right conditions.

❀ Some ferns, such as *Asplenium bulbiferum*, also reproduce by growing little plantlets or bulbils on their fronds. This particular fern needs a very sheltered position out of the sun and needs protecting in winter with a covering of straw or old fronds. It is probably better grown in a conservatory.

❀ Epiphytic ferns grow on trees, rocks or walls and draw their nutrients from rotting vegetation, which collects in the crevices.

❀ Almost all ferns require damp conditions if they are to thrive. A very few genera such as *Dryopteris* and *Osmunda* will tolerate dry conditions but only if well shaded. Many, such as *Allyrium* and *Osmunda*, die down at the first touch of frost so should not be grown in a winter interest garden. Some of the *Dryopteris* retain their fronds until well into winter. Leave the old fronds on the plant until early spring to protect the crown from frost but remove them as soon as the young fronds begin to unfurl.

RIGHT: *The feathery flower heads of the pink Astilbe 'Erica' associate well with the tall and stately Osmunda and Matteuccia ferns, growing happily in a semi-woodland situation.*

## Fern shapes

❀ Fern fronds comprise several basic shapes. There are triangular ferns, such as the five-fingered maidenhair fern (*Adiantum pedatum*), which has upright, lime-green fronds that die down in winter. They look attractive grown with other ferns in a shady border or woodland setting.

LEFT: *This very natural-looking woodland planting scheme has tiny alpine-type plants growing from crevices in the wall and a mixture of wild flowers and ferns against the hedgerow.*

❀ There are lance-shaped fronds, such as those found in the shuttlecock or ostrich fern (*Matteuccia struthiopteris*), whose fronds turn brown in late summer and persist for over a year, creating a striking display. These are among the most graceful of ferns and they deserve a prominent position in a shady part of the garden, perhaps at the top of steps or as an eye-catcher in a paved corner.

❀ Simple strap-like fronds are found in the hart's tongue fern (*Asplenium scolopendrium*), a very hardy evergreen fern with a crown of mid-green fronds. The crosiers look intriguingly like small green cobras when the dead fronds have been removed.

❀ Antler-shaped fronds are seen only in the staghorn ferns such as *Platycerium bifurcatum*, whose basal fronds are shaped like kidneys and reach up to 60 cm (24 in) and turn brown when fully grown. They form a shield around the base of the antler-like fronds, which grow up to 80 cm (32 in) long and remain green. These are tropical plants and suited only to greenhouse, conservatory or indoor cultivation.

BELOW: *This congregation of shade-loving plants includes the small bleeding heart* (Dicentra formosa)*, the* Dryopteris *fern, a large blue-green hosta and a purple* Cotinus.

## THE RIGHT CONDITIONS

FERNS are very tough and require the minimum of care and maintenance once established. Most ferns prefer neutral to alkaline conditions, and well-dug soil with added organic matter will suit most species.

❀ There are one or two that prefer acidic soil and which should be used in areas where other acidic soil lovers, such as rhododendrons and azaleas, grow. For example, the hard fern (*Blechnum spicant*), which has evergreen, leathery ladder-like fronds, is easier to grow in acidic soils, loves shady borders in woodland areas and associates well with acid-loving shrubs.

❀ The large ferns such as *Matteuccia* varieties will thrive in the damp conditions near ponds or streams. They associate well with large-leaved plants that love moisture, too, such as *Gunnera* and *Rodgersia* and reflect very prettily in still water.

### Ferns in formal settings

❀ Ferns can be used successfully in formal settings. For example, they can be planted in clumps or rows behind a very low clipped hedge of golden box bordered by woodland.

❀ The dark trees will highlight the feathery outline of the ferns, while the ferns themselves soften the hard edge of the box. They also look good when they are used formally in a courtyard or paved area in the corner of a garden that gets little sun.

❀ If growing ferns in pots you must make sure they are kept moist at all times. They look good grown near formal water features, especially where a little water is allowed to escape into the surrounding soil.

ABOVE: *Most ferns and primulas prefer soil that will not dry out. Here, the large shuttlecock fern (*Matteuccia struthiopteris*) mingles with a cerise candelabra primula (*Primula bulleyana*) to make a delightful combination.*

BELOW: *An enormous, clipped shrubby Lonicera hedge, shaped like a pillow, is brightened and enlivened by the bright green feathery leaves of a large clump of Dryopteris.*

## Ferns in rock crevices

✤ The lance-shaped fronds of the semi-evergreen *Ceterach officinarum* contrast well with the hard surfaces of the rock or brick that provides shelter and nutrients for them.

✤ If you build a double wall at the edge of a patio or front garden with a space in the middle for plants, these little ferns can be grown there, too, but remember that they should be in the shade.

## Naturalising ferns in woodland

✤ Although woodland may sound a bit grand, in a small garden one good-sized silver birch or a small clump of deciduous trees planted close together can count as woodland. Where ferns are concerned, the woodland needs to be moist most of the time.

✤ Ferns planted in drifts in woodland look very pretty but they need not be grown on their own. They associate very well with lilies and also with groups of broad-leaved hostas and spring bulbs such as wood anemones and bluebells.

✤ The male fern (*Dryopteris filix-mas*), which keeps most of its fronds throughout winter, is a very accommodating plant and thrives in shade but will tolerate full sun. It will even grow at the foot of a privet hedge. Like most hardy ferns, it forms solid clumps and looks very pretty grown in drifts among trees and woodland shrubs.

✤ The common polypody (*Polypodium vulgare*) is drought tolerant and adaptable. It spreads easily and makes good ground cover. It will also grow on rocks and trees. It has dark green, lance-shaped, deeply lobed fronds and spreads via green rhizomes, which eventually form mats. It prefers an acidic soil, as does *Blechnum spicant*, a fern with a distinctive rich green colour.

## Ferns as specimen plants

✤ Many ferns deserve a prominent position where they will be noticed and appreciated for some special quality. The Japanese painted fern *Athyrium niponicum* var. *pictum* is one of the prettiest, with metallic silver-grey fronds and purple midribs. It does not grow very tall, but put it in a moist, fertile soil and a sheltered position and it will thrive and look very pretty, particularly with small spring bulbs such as *Anemone blanda* and the charming little blue scillas and other small woodland plants.

✤ The royal fern (*Osmunda regalis*) is a large, stately fern growing to 1.5 m (5 ft) tall. It particularly likes waterside conditions in sun or shade. It makes a good container plant but must be regularly watered. It is best located near the house where it can be in a prominent position and its watering needs are less likely to be forgotten.

BELOW: *Foxgloves and ferns both grow in woodland conditions and associate well together under the canopy of deciduous trees.*

## USEFUL PLANT ASSOCIATIONS

ELEPHANT'S ears (*Bergenia*), with large, shiny, rounded evergreen leaves, can be a little dull on their own when not in flower.

They look much more interesting planted next to ferns, especially the feathery ones, such as the beech fern (*Phegopteris connectilis*), whose lime-green fronds contrast with the dark green of the *Bergenia*. *Bergenia* 'Silberlicht' has loose white flowers and is a more elegant and interesting variety than the more usual pink-flowering ones.

## WATER PLANTS

Water in the garden – whether a formal pool, a small stream, a short cascade or a wildlife pond – will allow you to grow many plants that do not thrive in any other conditions.

❀ Even in the smallest plot you can have a trough with dwarf water lilies floating in it. In a larger garden a formal or informal pond can create a strong focus and set the garden's style. It may incorporate a fountain or waterfall to create movement, sound and liveliness and water lilies will complete the scene.

❀ Floating plants, marginal, deep water and bog plants all add to the interest of a garden but need to be catered for carefully. Ponds should be made with shelves at different heights so that pond baskets can be put at the heights best suited to the various plants.

ABOVE: *This beautifully designed modern garden has a formal rectangular pond with a stone sculpture as a focal point. Water lilies float serenely on the calm surface of the water, and irises and other water-loving plants have been planted in the corners.*

BELOW: *This thoughtfully designed pond at the edge of a patio is planted with variegated hostas, which contrast with the large green-purple leaves of* Rodgersia, *the white and green strap-like leaves of* Phormium *and the slender leaves of a water iris.*

## Plants for formal ponds

❀ Plants with floating leaves and flowers, such as water lilies, are the obvious choice for formal pools. *Nymphaea* 'Froebelii' has deep red, starry flowers and purple-green rounded leaves; *N.* 'Marliacea Chromatella' is a yellow-flowered variety with olive green-streaked leaves.

❀ Arum lilies do not float but stand upright and look marvellous at the edge of a pond where their arrow-shaped leaves and pure white flowers can be reflected in the water. *Zantedeschia aethiopica* is the hardiest and will withstand several degrees of frost.

## Marginal plants

❀ Marginal plants are, in the main, very attractive plants grown at the edges of pools in shallow water about 7.5–15 cm (3–6 in) deep, but sometimes up to 30 cm (12 in) deep. Some species, such as water mint (*Mentha aquatica*) and *Veronica beccabunga*, also help to oxygenate the water.

❀ Ferns will grow well at the borders of informal pools and can form a good transition between a stream and the garden. Plants grown at pond margins also provide shelter for wildlife. *Iris laevigata* is tall and stately with fans of green, sword-like leaves and lavender-blue flowers.

❀ *Butomus umbellatus* has clusters of pale pink flowers in summer and early autumn and twisted bronze leaves. Purple loosestrife (*Lythrum salicaria*) has spires of reddish-purple flowers and lance-shaped leaves. The water forget-me-not (*Myosotis palustris*) has sky-blue flowers with yellow eyes all summer long.

❀ All these plants are valuable for breaking up the hard outline of a pond. In deeper marginal water you can grow the water flag (*Iris pseudacorus*), a tall, bright yellow variety of iris, but it may be too vigorous for smaller gardens.

## Bog and moisture-loving plants

❀ Numerous colourful plants will grow happily in soil that is kept permanently wet. The water violet (*Hottonia palustris*) has pale lilac flowers and likes full sun; *Anemone rivularis* has blue or white flowers from spring into summer; and ragged robin (*Lychnis floscuculi*) is a very pretty sharp pink flower with ragged petals, which used to be common and now seems to be rare in the wild.

❀ If you have room you could grow something on a grand scale such as *Gunnera tinctoria*, which has enormous, rhubarb-like leaves up to 1.5 m (5 ft) wide. Spikes of greenish-red flowers are followed by red or purple fruits.

❀ *Rodgersia aesculifolia* is another tall, stately plant with leaves like the horse chestnut tree and plumes of tiny, fragrant white flowers tinged with pink. *Rheum palmatum* also has large, handsome foliage and unusual flower spikes on reddish-purple stems.

# WATER GARDENS IN CONTAINERS

IN A small garden or a patio you can still have a pool without doing any construction work. Appropriate containers might be a sealed and lined half-barrel, a metal cauldron or a ceramic sink with the plughole stopped up. Although you will be able to grow only a few selected plants, the presence of even a little water can give great pleasure.

❀ Metal containers should be sealed with rubber paint or liner, otherwise the metal may be harmful to the plants and any fish you might want to keep. (If you do keep fish, they should be brought indoors over winter.) One suitable plant would be the tiny water lily, *Nymphaea pygmaea* 'Helvola', with pretty miniature yellow flowers. *N. tetragona* has white flowers no more than 5 cm (2 in) across and heart-shaped, dark green leaves.

LEFT: *The white skunk cabbage (*Lysichiton camtschatcensis*) is a marginal aquatic perennial, which flowers in early spring. Here, it is reflecting beautifully in the water.*

# INTRODUCING EXOTICS

Exotic plants are usually thought of as those from tropical and subtropical climates that find it hard to survive in temperate conditions. However, in mild areas such plants may grow quite happily in a sheltered part of the garden and, even in colder areas, many survive outside if protected over winter. Some are so tender that they need the protection of a greenhouse or conservatory even in the summer. However, some exotic-looking plants are perfectly hardy and not actually tropical. Exotics include many handsome architectural plants grown as focal points for their height and interesting shapes and foliage. They also include plants with highly colourful and unusual flowers and evergreens with a jungly look.

## CACTI AND SUCULENTS

CACTI and succulents come in an extraordinarily varied array of sizes, shapes, colours and textures. Many come from desert regions, where there is little rainfall and it gets very hot during the day and very cold at night.

❀ Some come from warm, humid rainforests. They have all adapted to their particular extreme conditions, turning their leaves, stems or roots into water storage tanks to help them withstand long periods of drought. Cacti differ from other succulents in having cushion-like growths on their stems from which spines, flowers and shoots develop.

❀ Succulents may have plump, smooth surfaces, a covering of silky hair or colourful spines. They may be symmetrical rosettes in shape or squat and globular or fluted like candlesticks. Many flower for only a short time and have large, brightly coloured flowers. Others flower for longer with many tiny blooms.

❀ In cool-temperate climates most cacti and succulents have to be grown in a conservatory or as houseplants, although there are some hardier species, which can make interesting garden displays. Nearly all need good drainage and will grow well in raised beds where the water can drain freely.

BELOW: *This secluded seating area has a wealth of container-grown succulents for colour and interest. Scented-leaved pelargoniums are fronted by the strong, spiky shapes of the Agave.*

ABOVE: *A row of succulents in terracotta pots sitting on a sunny wall by a patio will get the best of the daylight and warmth of the sun and will flourish accordingly.*

❀ Attractive collections of succulents can be grown outdoors in a relatively cool climate if you choose your varieties carefully. *Sedum* cultivars are often grown in mixed borders, although they usually look much more striking grown in a row or in swathes against a stone wall. There are some excellent deep purple varieties such as *S. spectabile* 'Abendrot'.

## Succulents in containers

❀ Most succulents have shallow roots and are therefore ideal for growing in containers. Wide, shallow containers are best for low-growing and creeping species such as the hardy *Sempervivum montanum*, a variety of houseleek, which makes neat little rosettes and is ideal for a trough garden.

❀ *Lewisia* varieties have brilliant little blooms on delicate stalks and also grow well in a trough or gravel garden, given a sheltered spot. Troughs are good for creating mixed planting of different sizes and habits.

❀ Large pots or urns are better for large plants with strap-like leaves such as *Agave attenuata*. A raised bed with shallow soil and plenty of gravel is also a good place to grow mixed succulent plantings.

## Succulents as focal points

❀ The agaves are spiky and statuesque. Grown in regions where the temperature seldom drops below freezing, *Agave parryi* has plump symmetrical rosettes of grey-green leaves and *Opuntia polyacantha* has brilliant yellow flowers. Each of these makes a splendid focal point on its own.

## Trailing succulents

❀ Several succulents have a trailing habit and can be stunning planted in hanging baskets. *Ceropegia woodii* produces waterfalls of brightly coloured flowers and can be used in warm, sunny courtyards or in conservatories.

RIGHT: *Bananas are satisfyingly exotic with their enormous, shiny green leaves, which become tattered as they grow older. This young banana, Musa acuminata, requires a sheltered spot.*

## ARCHITECTURAL EXOTICS

THERE are many splendid plants that can be grown for their architectural interest, to use as focal points and eye-catchers. Many are hardy; others can thrive in temperate climates, if they are given due care, attention and protection.

### Tree ferns

❀ Tree ferns are true ferns, and come from tropical forests. They have enormous upright rhizomes, which look like tree trunks and which can grow up to 4 m (13 ft). They are so stately that just one could be the only plant needed in a city courtyard.

❀ The Tasmanian tree fern (*Dicksonia antarctica*) will certainly not survive several cold winters in succession but, given a shady position where it is protected from the wind by a tall evergreen hedge, it may well survive many years.

❀ Temperate climates are not really humid enough for tree ferns so in summer spray the trunk or rig up an automatic system to water it. In warmer areas, winter protection may not be necessary but it certainly will be in cold rural areas.

❀ Overwinter your fern by surrounding the trunk with convenient insulating material such as polystyrene plant trays tied around the trunk. Fill the crown with straw and fix a hat of polystyrene on top. Stack straw bales around the trunk and fronds as high up as possible.

❀ Tree ferns become hardier the taller they grow so buy the tallest one you can find. Young plants with no trunk are not suitable to overwinter outdoors except in very sheltered spots.

### Yuccas

❀ Yuccas bring height and very exotic white blooms to the garden. Most are hardy enough for hot sunny sites in temperate climates. Use them as focal points in a border or on their own, or as effective eye-catchers on steps and terraces or in courtyards.

❀ If you want lots of lush growth, remove the yucca's spent flower spikes before they have fully faded as well as any dying or dead leaves. Some yuccas form a trunk and branch after flowering.

BELOW: *These purple phormiums, although they certainly look exotic, are reliably hardy in many temperate areas if grown in sheltered areas. In most places bananas should be taken indoors in winter.*

LEFT: *Despite its exotic, glamorous appearance, the yucca is surprisingly hardy and makes a spectacular statement, particularly as a feature in its own right.*

❀ *Trachycarpus* (fan palm) is a family of six species of evergreen palms from the temperate forests of subtropical Asia. They have a very attractive habit of growth with fan-shaped leaves and cup-shaped flowers. Fan palms are small enough to be grown in a courtyard but make splendid specimen trees in any garden. They like full sun or dappled shade and should be sheltered from cold, drying winds.

❀ The Chusan palm (*Trachycarpus fortunei*) is a single-stemmed palm with a head of fan-shaped, dark green leaves 45–75 cm (18–30 in) long, and small yellow flowers. Female plants have blue-black berries. It needs shelter, particularly from north and east winds.

❀ The dwarf fan palm (*Chamaerops humilis*) is a shrubby palm, which grows in Mediterranean regions. It has rosettes of long, graceful, finger-like leaves and tiny three-petalled flowers. It is a good specimen plant for a small garden. If there is danger of frost it is best grown in a pot and taken into a conservatory or indoors for winter.

❀ These include *Yucca floribunda*, *Y. gloriosa* (Spanish dagger), *Y. g.* 'Variegata' and *Y. recurvifolia*. Some form a clump of several plants without trunks. When one individual in the clump flowers, it dies and is replaced by a new plant from underneath. *Y. whipplei* may take many years to flower so grow it only for its leaves.

## Phormium

❀ These evergreen perennials come from New Zealand. They form striking clumps of large, strap-like leaves, ranging in colour from yellow-green to deep purple. They create spectacular focal points in a border, next to a building or at the edge of a lawn.

❀ They give a truly jungly feeling, although many are perfectly hardy. *Phormium tenax* 'Dazzler' has arching bronze leaves with red, orange and pink stripes and looks strong in a mainly red border. *P.* 'Sundowner' has bronze-green leaves; *P.* 'Variegatum' is light green with cream and lime stripes and looks good against darker foliage plants or a clipped hedge.

## Palms

❀ These stately trees always look wonderful swaying on the skyline in tropical countries. There are only two hardy palms and both can add an exotic feel to a garden. Grown in a border, they can give a truly splendid touch, or they may be grown as specimens on their own.

ABOVE: *These gardens at Tresco in the Scilly Isles have a remarkably mild climate, and many semi-tropical plants grow here that will not grow on the British mainland. Here, a tall palm gazes out over the other islands and an agave presides over smaller plants lower down the hill.*

# CULTIVATING GRASSES AND BAMBOOS

Grasses have become popular in gardens over the last few years for very good reasons. They have elegant and architectural forms, long seasons of interest and need little attention. They can also cope with a certain amount of drought, an invaluable quality in the modern garden. They bring movement and a luminous quality into garden planting as they sway in the wind and their leaves catch the sunlight.

## THE GRASS FAMILY

MEMBERS of the grass family (*Gramineae*), which includes bamboos, have rounded, hollow stems with regularly placed swellings or nodes from which the leaves appear. The flowers of grasses are small but are often held in large, showy panicles, spikes or plumes or stiff poker-like heads, well above the leaves.

Although they lack bright colours, their golds, browns, greens and yellows catch the sun, producing beautiful subtle effects. Their arching stems, feathery flowers and subtle colouring can create marvellous displays, whether used as individual specimens or grouped together. Many have attractive flowers and seed heads that appear in midsummer and last well into winter.

### The tall and the short

Large grasses are admired for their statuesque quality and feather-duster plumage. Unfortunately, the overuse of the very tall and stately pampas grass (*Cortaderia selloana*) has given grass a bad name. It is undeniably beautiful in the right setting but at one time it seems to have been planted in almost every suburban garden as a matter of course, where it was out of proportion, out of keeping

BELOW: *The strap-like leaves of this purple phormium and the narrower leaves of the grasses go particularly well together, providing interesting movement and light for those sitting on the bench.*

ABOVE: *Although the leaves of the grasses* Imperata cylindrica '*Rubra*' *and* Roscoea scillicifolia *have a similar strap-like quality, variety is provided in good measure by the colours, which light up when the sun shines on them.*

## CHOOSING GRASSES

IT is important to choose the right grasses for a particular effect. Clump-forming upright growers, such as varieties of *Calamagrostis*, will preside over lower-growing plants but lose all impact if crowded by plants of equal height. More open grasses, such as *Paricum virgatum* with loose flower and seed heads, can be used with taller perennials because of their almost transparent quality.

❧Colour is important, too. If you grow the luminous green *Milium effusum* 'Aureum' in front of a bed next to the lawn, it will simply look like another bit of green grass. Choose the blue grass *Festuca glauca* instead, and it will contrast with the lawn grass very effectively.

### Grasses by the sea

❧Almost all grasses are invaluable grown in coastal or seaside gardens. Their ethereal quality seems to match that of the sea; they can cope well with wind and salt spray and are at home in a sandy and pebbly environment. The taller ones can be used for structure, the smaller ones for foliage, colour and for filling gaps.

and badly maintained. It is indeed a regal plant but only for a very large garden or for planting in quantity by a lakeside or as a feature.

❧ *C. selloana* is the hardiest pampas grass but there are many more rewarding grasses to choose for the smaller garden. Choose *Miscanthus sinensis* 'Silberfeder' (silver feather), or M. '*Zebrinus*', whose arching green leaves are intriguingly striped yellow. *Pinnisetum alopecuroides* has brown, caterpillar-shaped flower heads and can be grown in clumps under deciduous trees. Smaller grasses are more useful for their foliage effect, both in form and colour.

❧ Varieties of *Festuca*, *Milium*, *Elymus* and *Carex* are all excellent foliage plants and extremely useful in a border. They associate well with small perennials, dwarf conifers and shrubs, contributing a hedgehog roundness but feather softness that contrasts well with the upright shape of many perennials. Most are evergreen and so provide interest for the whole year.

RIGHT: *The tall, feathery stems of* Stipa gigantea *with the lower-growing* Miscanthus sinensis '*Silberfeder*' *and the fiery red of* Crocosmia '*Bressingham Blaze*' *make a really striking combination.*

ABOVE: *Grasses can look especially picturesque in a winter border after a heavy frost; they can lend a magical quality to an otherwise bland and colourless area.*

### Grasses in the mixed border

❀ Many mixed borders will benefit from grasses grown among the shrubs and herbaceous perennials. *Stipa gigantea* is useful because its pale yellow stems and flowers make a significant shape but it is sparse enough for other plants to be seen through it. Its pale straw-like colour goes well with many of the later summer flowers such as *Echinaceae purpurea*, *Crocosmia* 'Lucifer' and *Aster amellus* 'King George'.

❀ Low-growing grasses look good at the front of mixed borders. Choose the tufted ones that build up slowly from a central crown. *Festuca glauca* 'Elijah blue' is evergreen and has vivid blue, needle-like leaves and blue-grey plumes of flowers in early summer. Vigorous, creeping grasses are not suitable for borders. *Phalaris arundinacea*, for example, will simply smother weaker plants growing nearby and will require endless weeding.

### Grasses in winter borders

❀ When many flowers have died down for the winter, the grasses can come into their own, keeping a border alive when it has lost its summer and autumn colour. They can look spectacular when caught by a heavy frost so that their seed heads and leaves are outlined with a sugar icing coating.

❀ Taller grasses associate well with the sea hollies such as *Eryngium agavifolium*, whose seed heads continue to be attractive in winter, and also with *Sedum* 'Autumn Joy', whose flat plates of heads last well into winter, too, and contrast with the feathery heads of grass. In a large border the larger grasses look great with the seed heads of cardoons (*Cynara cardunculus*).

### Grasses for paved areas and patios

❀ Some of the smaller grasses are suitable for growing between paving slabs. Purple moor grass (*Molinia caerulea*) has slender green upright leaves, which form into mounds with open panicles of purple flowers in summer. It will tolerate acidic, boggy soils, so can be used near pools.

❀ For a warm patio area try *Helictotrichon sempervirens* in a bed sheltered by a wall. Its slender blue leaves are upright and radiate stiffly so it looks suitably architectural next to a building.

### Water's edge grasses

❀ *Glyceria aquatica* 'Variegata' has an attractive form, tolerates shade and spreads slowly. *Phragmites australis* is a tall species. It needs moist soil and will grow well by a pond or stream.

ABOVE: *The tall, feathery plumes of pampas grass* Cortaderia selloana *'Sunningdale Silver' give a spectacular display, which contrasts with the paddle-shaped leaves and bright red flowers of* Canna *'President'.*

### Areas dedicated to grass

❀ If you have enough space, you might like to have a grass garden, creating your own area of American prairie. Varieties of *Cortaderia* and *Miscanthus* make a striking display. They are best grown in an open position where they will get the benefit of sun on their foliage and flowers and the wind will set them swaying.

## SEDGES, RUSHES AND CAT'S TAILS

THESE plants are often confused with grasses but each belongs to a separate family. Although they will grow in sun or shade, they must have moist soil and are mostly useful for the bog garden.

❀ Sedges are grown for their attractive foliage. They thrive in bog conditions but are often tolerant of dryer sites. The flowers are grouped into spikelets, which may be richly coloured.

❀ The variegated species can offer good colour contrasts in a border. Members of the *Carex* family form dense mounds of evergreen hair-like leaves. *Carex* 'Bronze Form' has matt brown leaves, while those of *C. elata* 'Aurea' are bright yellow with narrow green edges.

❀ The rush family (*Juncaceae*) includes the rushes and the woodrushes, all of which have attractive leaves. Like sedges, they should be grown in a bog garden or a bed whose soil is reliably moist. The rushes prefer shade and make good ground cover plants. *Juncus effusus* 'Spiralis' has tiny brown flowers in loose clusters. Snowy woodrush (*Luzula nivea*) has light green leaves in loose tufts with clusters of white flowers in summer and will tolerate sun.

❀ Cat's tails are deciduous with invasive rhizomes. *Typha latifolia* is the common bulrush or reed mace, whose brown flower heads are poker shaped and topped with thin spikes. It is often seen growing in rivers or streams but it can be invasive. *T. minima* (dwarf reed mace) is less so and has dark brown flower spikes in summer.

BELOW: *Grasses and sedges are particularly striking when the frost catches them on a bright winter's morning. The grassy meadow by this wooden bridge has a silver frosty sheen, against which the dark pokers of the bulrushes stand out strikingly.*

## BAMBOOS

BAMBOOS belong to the grass family (*Gramineae*). They are evergreen with woody hollow stems called culms and narrow, handsome foliage. Bamboos make excellent architectural plants; even when used as screens or hedges, they make a dramatic statement in any garden.

✿ They will grow in any dry, sheltered, shady spot and can create a lush tropical effect together with other evergreen shrubs. The tall vertical culms make interesting contrasts with the fronded foliage of ferns. Japanese anemones can be grown nearby, especially white ones such as *Anemone* x *hybrida* 'Honorine Joubert'.

✿ Most bamboos need plenty of space, since the larger ones will grow up to 4 m (13 ft) tall and many arch over 6 m (20 ft), but there are also some dwarf species.

✿ Some bamboos form clumps and make good specimen plants or focal points. Others have running rhizomes and need to be contained, unless grown in a wild garden or as ground cover. Canes can be green, brown, black, yellow, pink or purple, mottled or streaked. Do not expect bamboos to bloom, however. It may take 100 years for flowers to appear. On the whole, the flowers are untidy anyway and bamboos look better without them.

✿ Bamboos need a sheltered spot, protected from the wind, or they will lose excessive water. Although fully hardy, a bamboo in a container can suffer from drought in winter and it is wise to insulate the pot with fleece or plastic bubble wrap.

✿ Bamboos grow strongly in most soils once they have become established, and some spread very quickly. Many are tropical but plenty are hardy in temperate regions. They can be grown in beds in the garden or in tubs on roofs or in container gardens. A grove or specimen plant of bamboos can transform a prim garden into a much more mysterious and interesting area.

### Bamboos in containers

✿ Bamboos can look superb when well grown in large containers. Terracotta and glazed Chinese pots are suitable but the plants can look just as stately grown in galvanised bins and buckets. The invasive, running types of bamboo are certainly best grown in pots, particularly in small gardens, otherwise they may spread and become a nuisance.

ABOVE: *If you have a small garden, but like the look of bamboo, many small varieties can be kept in a smaller container. Alternatively, you can achieve a similar effect with a Cyperus like the one above.*

✿ Bamboos are thirsty, hungry plants. Failure to water them sufficiently will cause the leaves to turn brown and even loss of nearly all the leaves. Once this has happened, they will be slow to recover. More vigorous and invasive species will fill up their containers in no time with rhizomes and roots and will then use up water and nutrients at an alarming rate.

✿ Such plants should be repotted every year but there are species that are more suitable for containers. These are slower growing and some may be kept in the same pot for five years or more. *Chimonobambusa marmorea* grows to 1.5 m (5 ft) and is a semi-dwarf Japanese variety with tightly bunched leaves. *C. marmorea* 'Variegata' has thin reddish stems and yellow striped leaves.

ABOVE: *This very Japanese scene includes a bamboo fence with the slim, black-stemmed bamboo* Phyllostachys nigra *growing against it, a stone lantern and two small hummocks of the low-growing blue grass* Festuca glauca *'Elijar Blue'.*

### Bamboos in a Japanese garden

✤ Bamboos are more or less essential in a Japanese garden. Tall varieties such as *Fargesia murieliae*, which grows to 4 x 1.5 m (13 x 5 ft) and is particularly elegant as a specimen plant, can conceal the edge of a small garden, making it look much larger.

✤ A gravel area with a stone lantern on it will be given extra atmosphere by this arching plant. *F. m.* 'Simba' reaches only half the height or less and might suit a small garden better.

### Interesting stems

✤ Some bamboos have striking stems, which are as much of a feature as their leaves. Plant these where the stems will really be noticed, rather than in some forgotten corner of the garden. They will look good in containers in a small area or as focal points and can be used as screens where they will please the eye while concealing what lies behind.

✤ Such bamboos include *Phyllostachys edulis*, whose distinctive culms are covered in a waxy white powder, which makes them look white. *P. nigra* has elegant, narrow ebony-black stems and is a very good variety for smaller gardens.

### Ground cover bamboos

✤ A few bamboos can be used for ground cover. *Pleioblastus pygmaeus* (syn. *Arundinaria pygmaea*) is a dwarf bamboo with fern-like leaves with very slender culms. It looks attractive grown in a shallow container.

LEFT: *Bamboos have many uses in the garden and the canes, or culms, can provide as much interest as the foliage. This one is* Clusquea couleou, *which forms dense clumps of yellow-green to olive-green canes and will grow to 6 m (20 ft) tall.*

# INDEX